THE ILLUSTRATED

EGYPTIAN

BOOK

OF THE

DEAD

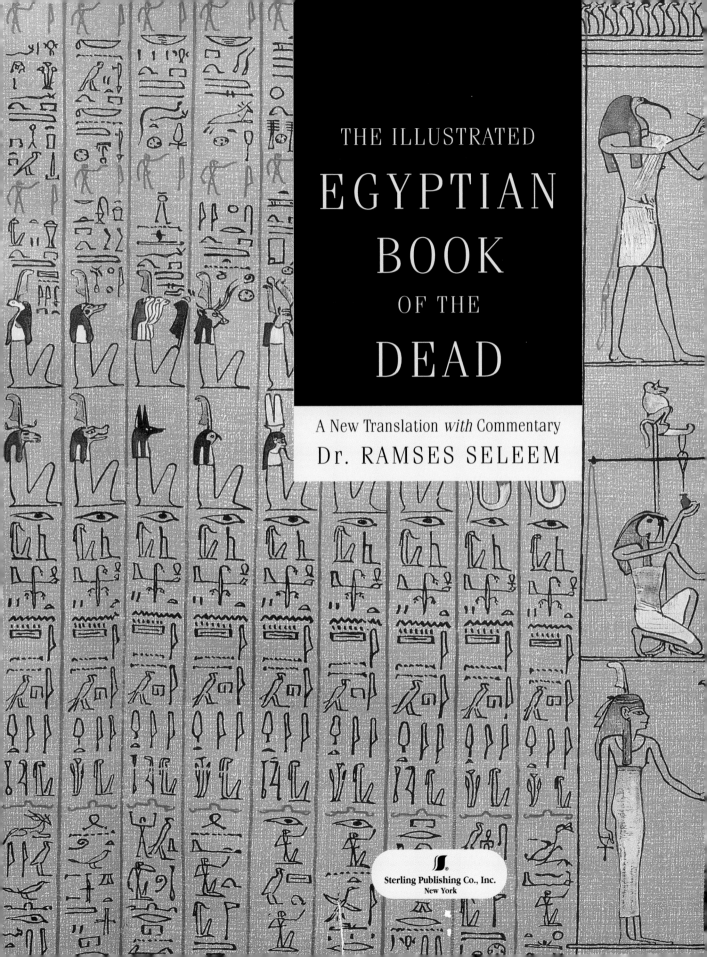

THE ILLUSTRATED
EGYPTIAN
BOOK
OF THE
DEAD

A New Translation *with* Commentary
Dr. RAMSES SELEEM

Sterling Publishing Co., Inc.
New York

Library of Congress Cataloging-in-Publication Data Available

10 9 8 7 6 5 4 3 2 1

Published in 2001 by Sterling Publishing Company, Inc.
387 Park Avenue South, New York, N.Y. 10016
© 2001 Godsfield Press
Text © 2001 Dr Ramses Seleem

Dr Ramses Seleem asserts the moral right to be
identified as the author of this work.

Distributed in Canada by Sterling Publishing
c/o Canadian Manda Group, One Atlantic Avenue, Suite 105
Toronto, Ontario, Canada M6K 3E7
Distributed in Australia by Capricorn Link (Australia) Pty Ltd
P. O. Box 6651, Baulkham Hills, Business Centre, NSW 2153, Australia

Printed and bound in China

Sterling ISBN 0-8069-2659-7

To my son, Heru, so that he may walk with the masters of eternity.

CONTENTS

Preface   6

1   Introduction   8

2   The Symbolism of the Egyptian Medu-Netru   34

3   The Papyrus of Hunefer: Illustrations and Translation   46

4   Extracts from *The Book of the Dead*   102

    Extracts from the Papyrus of Enhai   104

    Extracts from the Papyrus of Gerusher (*The Book of Breathings*)   108

    Extract from the Papyrus of the Royal Mother Nezemt:

    The Negative Confessions   114

    Extracts from the Papyrus of Ani   120

Afterword   138

Glossary   140

Index   142

Author Biography   144

PREFACE

The Papyrus of Hunefer was found at Thebes (Uast) in Egypt and bought by the British Museum from Clot Bey in 1852. Measuring 18 ft. x 1 ft. 3⅜ in., it is considered to be the shortest text of *The Book of the Dead*, dating from the Theban period.

In this book, I have translated the entire Papyrus of Hunefer, and Chapters 1 and 2 of the Papyrus of Ani, as well as extracts from the Papyrus of Enhai, the Papyrus of Gerusher, and the Negative Confessions of the Papyrus of the Royal Mother Nezemt. I have also divided the translation into numbered sentences for ease of reference, although these do not exist in the original texts because the Egyptian contains no punctuation of any kind.

I hope that this humble work will help you in your path to studying the sacred knowledge of the Egyptians, and will shed new light on the true meaning and profound structure of this body of knowledge.

With showers of blessings.

Dr. Ramses Seleem
London, 2000

The colossal statues that stand before the temple of Emen in the Valley of the Kings. Greek travelers recorded that these statues used to sing a hymn at sunrise and sunset. The temple of Emen was the largest of all the Egyptian temples in that area, but it was destroyed and all that remains today are these two statues.

— 1 —
INTRODUCTION

I n the 18th dynasty of the ancient Egyptian empire, Kha-M-Hat carved a
message to future generations at the entrance of the inner chamber of his
tomb. The inscription began with the words, "O you, both great and small,
who will be on earth, O scribes, who can decipher difficult writings and are
skilled in the Medu-Netru (hieroglyphs), you who set out in search of all kinds
of knowledge, you who blissfully enjoy your achievements, all who will pass
through this chapel that I have built as a place of rest for the blessed, who will
contemplate these walls and read my words aloud..."

INTRODUCTION

In the Papyrus of Ani, Ani (the chief scribe of the Pharaoh, Seti I) says:

See, is it not written in this scroll? Read, you who will discover it in future ages, if God has given you the power to read. Read, children of the future, and learn the secrets of the best, which are so distant to you and yet in reality so near. Men do not live once, in order to vanish forever. They live several lives in different places but not always in this world, and between each life there is a veil of shadows. The doors will finally open and we shall see all the places where our feet have trodden since the dawn of time. Our religion teaches us that we live for eternity. Thus, since eternity has no end, it cannot have a beginning. It is a circle. If, therefore, the one is true, namely that we live eternally, the other must also be true, namely that we have always lived. In the eyes of men, God has many faces and each swears he has seen the true and only God. Yet it is not so, for all of these faces are merely the face of God. Our Ka, which is our double, reveals them to us in different ways. By drawing from the bottomless well of wisdom, which is hidden in the essence of every man, we perceive grains of truth, which give those of us with knowledge the power to perform marvelous things.

The Egyptian religious texts contain all the spiritual doctrines that every human being aspires to learn. *The Book of Coming Forth by Day*, which was named *The Book of the Dead* by Egyptologists, describes the future of the soul after death in the intermediate world. This world was known as the Dwat by the ancient Egyptians, or the netherworld or purgatory state by Catholics. The ancient Egyptians believed that there were three worlds: the world below, Ta, the world above, Nut, and the world in between, Dwat. The soul travels from the realm of Ta (earth) to the realm of Dwat (netherworld), and finally to the spiritual realm of Nut (heaven), either to be born again or to become one with the perfected souls who are not subject to the reincarnation laws. A full explanation of the realm of the Dwat was given in *The Book of M-Dwat* or "What is in the Dwat."

Although this work was originally called *The Book of Coming Forth by Day*, it has become more popularly known as *The Book of the Dead*, so this is the name we will use in the rest of this book.

Ancient Egyptians believed that Tehuty wrote *The Book of the Dead* 50,000 years ago. The compositions of the chapters of *The Book of the Dead* are only a portion of the books written by Tehuty.

The Book of the Dead is composed of rescensions, whose purpose was to be read and enacted by the living, in order to help the living and the dead in their journey through the netherworld. It was to ensure that they could find their way to the spiritual realm, and be saved from the darkness of the Dwat, and to reach the Fields of Earu, or The Garden of Reeds, where true peace envelops the soul.

The texts themselves embody a great deal of knowledge, since they incorporate many aspects of the ancient Egyptian symbolism. I have divided the text into numbered sentences, so that each can be identified and studied individually. Before beginning the study of the actual texts, however, there are some significant points that require explanation.

The ancient Egyptians did not worship many gods and goddesses, as is commonly believed. This misconception arose from the mistranslation of the words *Neter* and *Netrit* as "god" and "goddess" respectively. The word *Neter*, in fact, means principle or law, masculine, while *Netrit* means principle or law, feminine. Both words, therefore, refer to the natural laws governing creation, rather than deities. *Neter* and *Netrit* are very similar in meaning to the "yin" and "yang" of Chinese philosophy.

Another common misconception is that the ancient Egyptians spent their time worshiping idols of cats, dogs, scarabs, or humans, or kneeling before them.

A basic comprehension of the ancient Egyptian spiritual doctrine is necessary to understand *The Book of the Dead*. We should be aware that Egyptian mythology is the foundation of all Egyptian ritual. Mythology is considered the earth of eternity; rituals are the earth of time. The Egyptian sages expressed their teachings by symbolic and sometimes mythological figures, thereby avoiding the use of technical diagrams, classifications, and theoretical speculation.

The divine qualities in nature are reflections of the natural laws or Netru, and they are part of the self.

Nut (heaven) in the form of a woman stretching out her arms and legs around the horizons. In Egyptian mythology it says, "Nut swallows the sun disc at the end of the day and gives birth to it the second day younger than yesterday."

These divine qualities can be learned by studying the Egyptian Kher (philosophy), symbolism, and images, and by observing their effects in nature.

The Book of the Dead is quite lengthy—189 chapters. It is important to me to represent it accurately from the point of view of the ancient Egyptians, since previous attempts by other authors have tended to be colored by the speculative theories of Egyptologists, which can often be misleading.

The Book of the Dead is the only living record of the twofold mystery—the mystery of life and death. It is considered by many to be the pre-Christian word of God. The spiritual concepts contained in *The Book of the Dead* explain life in its continuity and the condition of the reincarnated soul both in this life and in the Dwat. This is in direct contrast to the emphasis on death and dead relics that can often be seen in modern museums. The concepts embodied in *The Book of the Dead* were embraced by the religious and philosophical system of the Taoists, the Oriental religion and philosophy of Buddhism; Druidism, the religion of the ancient Celts; Kabbalism, the ancient tradition of Jewish mysticism; the ancient Persian religion of Mazdaism or Zoroastrianism; and Gnosticism, a synthesis of Christianity, Greek Philosophy, Hinduism, and other religious beliefs, popular in the 2nd and 3rd centuries BCE.

Many great people were also either educated in Egypt or spent time there. These included Moses, the ancient Hebrew prophet, and the ancient Greek philosophers Pythagoras, Plato, and Thales, as well as the statesman and lawyer, Solon, and the epic poet, Homer. However, it is wiser to concentrate on the roots of all spiritual conceptions and ignore the branches and leaves, which cannot be understood without comprehension of the roots themselves.

An example of the correlation between the Egyptian and Western concepts is to be found in Chapter 90 of *The Book of the Dead*, where it is written:

O you, who restores memory in the mouth of the dead through the words of power, which they possess, let my mouth be opened through the words of power, which I possess.

Ptah, the immortal who ruled Egypt for 9,000 years, and who was the originator of art. From the tomb of Horemheb.

The judgment scene, where the deceased is standing in the hall of justice before the 42 natural laws. Enpu (Anubis) is holding the scales of justice where the deeds of the deceased are weighed against the feather of truth, and Tehuty (Hermes) is writing the outcome of the judgment.

This reflects the belief that the mouth of the dead person is opened for him by Ptah (the first craftsman) and Tum (son of Ptah), while Tehuty supplies him with the great words of power, which open every gate. This corresponds to the teachings of Plato, which say that knowledge of past lives can be acquired by breathing exercises, which recall the memory of the soul.

The Book of the Dead is, in reality, the Egyptian book of life—life now, life hereafter, and life everlasting. A copy was buried with the deceased to give the soul the tools to secure his or her future in the life hereafter.

The deceased entered Ementet (the land of the dead) with a papyrus scroll in one hand. The question that lay ahead was how well the deceased person had established truth in his or her lifetime against the powers of evil. The text buried with the deceased was written by Tehuty, the greatest educator of all humankind. On the day of judgment, Tehuty weighed this text against one written by the deceased during his or her lifetime on earth, to see how the individual's book of deeds measured up against the book of the truth, and every act was weighed on the balancing scales of justice.

Enpu (Anubis) performs the mummification procedures over the body of Oser (Osiris). Enpu was the son of Nebt-Het and was considered to be the guardian of hidden knowledge and the barrier between the visible and the invisible.

The questions that confronted the deceased in Ementet (the land of the dead) were:

- Did the deceased embrace life enough to be able to live again in death?
- Did the deceased develop a strong enough character, to continue his or her personality?
- Is the heart of the deceased person truly open spiritually?
- How many seeds of eternity did the deceased plant in his or her lifetime?
- Did the deceased apply enough effort to surpass physical limits (i.e. the man who broke his own egg, in the Egyptian myth)?
- Did the deceased make an effort to acquire possession of their eternal soul?
- Did the deceased make the words of truth a reality in everyday life by practicing them?

The religion of Egypt was not built on the life and personality of a single individual or prophet, but was built upon natural laws. The Egyptian salvation was based on truthfulness and a person's behavior during his or her lifetime. That's what acquired victory in Ementet (the land of the dead). It was the responsibility of the living to acquire power by achieving unity with their organs and making the house of life (the body) full of light, so that they could live eternally. As the texts of the 6th dynasty said, *"Live your life and you will never die."* In *The Book of the Dead*, it is written:

"I know in my heart that I have gained power over my emotions, I have gained power over my arms, I have gained power over my legs, and I have gained the power to do what pleases my spirit. My soul, therefore, shall not be imprisoned in my body and I shall enter the netherworld in peace and come forth in peace."

Knowledge gives the power to act in truth and causes life, while ignorance blinds the sight and causes death. As Tehuty said, *"Death is the result of ignorance alone."* A human being needs a map in order to travel, both in this lifetime and beyond. However, it is important not to confuse the map with the territory. A map of England is not England. How can you travel in life after death, without knowing the way?

The roads, ways, gates, hours, laws, and guardians of life after death are explained in detail in *The Book of the Dead*. And even though a copy of the book is buried with the deceased, it is better to learn this divine knowledge by heart and live it in this lifetime, so the words can become flesh (truth). Only then does *The Book of the Dead* in this life become the book of life in death. As Tehuty said, *"The wickedness of the soul is ignorance and the virtue of the soul is knowledge."* Human beings must become enlightened in order to find their way in the dark. Becoming enlightened means becoming smart travelers who acquire knowledge of the way, an understanding of the local language, and friendship with other travelers. We are all travelers in eternity and so we all require true initiation in this knowledge. The ancient Egyptians looked at life as an eternal journey. They understood that everyone was born with a different amount of spiritual awareness, depending on the soul's efforts in past lives.

Heru (Horus the Younger), the son of Est (Isis) and Oser (Osiris) said, *"I utter His words (the words of God) to the humans of the present generation and I repeat His words to him who is deprived of breath."* Oser trusted and knew without doubt that freedom from total destruction could be assured by mastering the lessons in *The Book of the Dead*.

Heru (Horus), the son of Oser (Osiris), wearing the red and white crown of north and south Egypt. He holds in his right hand the Uast scepter as a symbol of authority, and in his left hand the Ankh as a symbol of life.

The Ancient Egyptian Concepts of God and the Creation

Distorted ideas and misconceptions about Ancient Egyptians began to take hold after the collapse of the Egyptian Empire in 525 BCE. Thereafter, Egyptians were accused of being polytheistic: the Pharaohs were often perceived as tyrannical and corrupt, the priests as manipulative and lacking conviction, and the entire spiritual structure of ancient Egypt came to be regarded by many as pagan. These ideas, unfortunately, still persist in the minds of some people today.

In fact, ancient Egyptians believed in one God without name, gender, shape, or form. They gave this great, supreme power—which made the earth, heavens, seas, sky, men and women, animals, birds, and creeping things, and all that is and all that will be—the names Emen-Ra ("the hidden light"), Atum-Ra ("the source and end of all light"), and Eaau ("power that has been polarized and expanded, creating the universe"). As mentioned previously, Egyptologists fell victim to the mistranslation of the words *Neter* (meaning natural law, masculine) and *Netrit* (meaning natural law, feminine) as "god" and "goddess" respectively. These two words are, in reality, similar to the ancient Chinese concepts of "yin" and "yang."

Since all of nature is governed by a masculine or feminine law, it became very difficult for scholars to classify all the "gods" and "goddesses" because everything had become one or the other: the ant, dog,

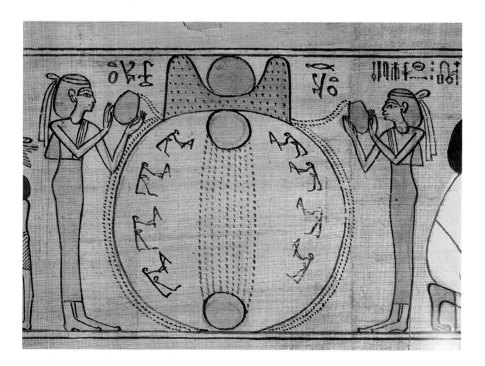

A depiction of the northern and southern heaven with the sun in between, traveling between the two horizons and giving life to all creations. A papyrus from the New Kingdom, c. 11th/12th century BCE.

jackal, falcon, and everything else. Indeed, Wallis Budge, in his book *The Gods of the Egyptians*, came across so many "gods" and "goddesses" that he created a whole chapter on "Miscellaneous Gods." The error is clear but some scholars today remain unaware of the truth. Too many western scholars of the 18th, 19th, and early 20th centuries arrogantly believed that their civilization was the most advanced. They tended to dismiss ancient cultures as superstitious, barbaric, primitive, uncivilized, and sometimes weird. Wallis Budge, in his translation of *The Egyptian Book of the Dead*, under the title *The Legend of Osiris*, wrote:

The chief features of the Egyptian religion remained unchanged from the 5th and 6th Dynasties down to the period when the Egyptians embraced Christianity, after the preaching of St. Mark the Apostle in Alexandria, in 69 CE, so firmly had the early beliefs taken possession of the Egyptian mind; and the Christians in Egypt, or Copts as they are commonly called, the racial descendants of the ancient Egyptians, seem never to have succeeded in divesting themselves of the superstitious and weird mythological conceptions which they inherited from their heathen ancestors.

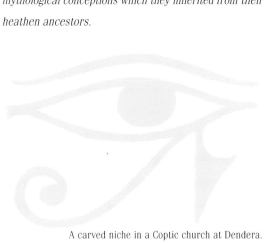

A carved niche in a Coptic church at Dendera.

A golden sunset, which represented death and resurrection in the Egyptian tradition.

Yet in his book *The Gods of the Egyptians* (page 133), Budge said: "It is easy to see from the hieroglyphic extract (given above) that to the Gods there described are attributed many of the creative qualities which we assign to God almighty." He continues, saying (page 137) that "the priests and theologians saw nothing incompatible in believing that God was one and that he existed under innumerable forms."

E. de Rougé says in an article (*Revue Archéologique*, 1860, page 73): "The unity of a supreme and self-existent being, his eternity, his almightiness, and eternal reproduction thereby as god; the attributing of the creation of the world and of all living beings to the supreme God; the immortality of the soul, completed by the dogma of punishments and rewards; such is the sublime and persistent base which, notwithstanding all deviations and all mythological embellishment, must secure for the beliefs of the ancient Egyptians a most honorable place among the religions of antiquity."

Mariette Bey, in his description of the principal monuments on display at the Egyptian Museum at Bûlâk in Cairo, said: "At the head of the Egyptian pantheon soars a God who is one, immortal, uncreated, invisible, and hidden in the inaccessible depths of his essence; he is the creator of the heavens and of the earth; he has made everything which exists and nothing has been made without him; such is the God who is reserved for the initiated of the sanctuary."

In the *Calendrier des Jours Fastes et Néfastes* (page 107), Chabas said: "The one God, who existed before all things, who represents the pure and abstract idea of divinity, is not clearly specialized by (any) one single personage of the vast Egyptian pantheon. Neither Ptah, nor Seb, nor Thoth, nor Ra, nor Osiris, nor any other god is a personification of him at all times; but of these sometimes one and at other times another is invoked in terms which assimilate these intimately with the supreme type; the innumerable gods of Egypt are only attributes and different aspects of this unique type."

Dr. Brusch, too, in his book *Religion und Mythologie* (page 96ff) indicated that the Egyptians themselves held that the gods were only names of the various attributes of the one God. As Tehuty said, *"None of our thoughts are capable of conceiving God, nor any language of defining Him, that which is incorporeal, formless, invisible, cannot be grasped by our senses. That which is eternal cannot be measured by the short rules of time. God is, accordingly, ineffable."*

In Chapter 154 of *The Book of the Dead*, the deceased king, Tehuty-mes III, praised God, saying:

Preserve me behind you, O Atum (God), from decay, like the fate that you have ordained for all masculine and feminine laws of nature, for all animals, and for all creeping things. For each, his soul goes forth after his death and he ascends after passing away.

Atum-Ra, the principle of light, with the deceased emerging from a sycamore tree over the back of a cow. This implies that the soul of the deceased is incarnated as different life forms and emerges through heaven.

Emen-Ra, the principle of hidden light, gives life to the Egyptian king during the ceremony of the festival of the tail.

The Egyptians believed that God manifested himself through His creations, sending His light to us via the sun disk, Eten. This light, which gives life to all forms of existence in nature, is called Ra, or the divine light of the right eye of God (the Sun). The ancient texts reveal the firm belief in one almighty God, who created everything. For example:

At the beginning of time, He created the two Paut (the two groups of nine laws). He brought into existence all the natural laws. Through Him, the one and only divine creator, He created all that exists, at the beginning of earthly life in primeval times. He is the creator of all mysteries and the multitude of forms, and His identity is unknown.

All forms of existence were made manifest by the power of the Netru, or the natural laws. There are 42 natural laws, nine of which are the principle laws, called Paut Netru, sometimes known as the Paut, or the Great Nine Laws. These were known by the Greeks as the Ennead and today, in different forms, they are commonly called the Enneagram. The Paut are the main laws of nature which function in the human psyche, according to the ancient college of Ennu (Heliopolis).

Atum-Ra (God, the source and end of all light) existed before there was any notion of space or time. This power wanted to make itself known and so it uttered the sacred word to create (sound). This in turn led to the creation of the primordial water of Nu, or the celestial ocean, which contained everything on the earth in an embryonic form. Nu was shrouded in darkness and contained the male and female forms of absolutely everything that was to exist in the future.

Atum-Ra felt the desire to begin the work of creation and uttered the sacred word to create. This sound brought the world to life, in the form of an egg, out of the water of Nu. From this egg came forth the light of God, which caused all forms of life to come into existence. Ra, the light of God in nature, was later manifest on earth through the disk of the sun, Aten, and appeared for the first time in the form of Dsher, or the sunrise at the beginning of life upon earth.

When light came forth upon earth for the first time, vanquishing darkness, the first humans were created. These took the form of eight primordial humans, four of which were male and four female, and they came into being when water fell from heaven (the tears of God, who cried for all future humans) and mixed with the soil of earth. These eight primordials of mankind were depicted as four male and four female baboons, who sang to the Creator upon the rising of the sun. They were also depicted as humans; the males with the heads of frogs and the females with the heads of cobras, symbolizing that they were immortal.

The eight primordials were, in reality, four couples, and they were created in Etelenty.

Kek and Keket

Kek and Keket were the first couple to be created, and were the elders of Etelenty. Their names signify darkness and their offspring were the black race. They were born at dusk.

Heh and Hehet

Heh and Hehet were the second couple to be created. They were known as the dawn people since their creation was at dawn. Their offspring were the Asian race.

Nun and Nunit

Nun and Nunit were the forefathers of the European peoples. They were born at midday.

Emen and Emenet

Emen and Emenet were the forefathers of the Egyptians. They were born at sunrise.

Among the offspring of the eight primordials was Tehuty, who carried the divine intelligence within him. Tehuty brought language and divine speech into existence, and his words explained and foretold the future of mankind. His words and knowledge became commands, and his commands became reality through the efforts of Ptah, the first craftsman on earth, who instructed artists in all forms of art, and Khnemu, the first master builder, who developed the life of mankind through his divine work of architecture. Ptah and Khnemu brought Tehuty's commands to fruition, and we marvel at the remnants of their work still to be seen today in the land of Egypt.

There was no evil in Etelenty, and the men and women who lived there followed the laws of nature. Since the creation process was not yet complete, the inhabitants of Etelenty saw the creation of the moon out of the soil of the Atlantic Ocean, and the creation of plants, animals, birds, and creeping things. The earth, however, was unstable and so Tehuty, knowing that Etelenty would be submerged by the ocean, ordered the emigration of the four families that formed the population of Etelenty.

The emigration of these four families took place more than 50,000 years ago. The family of Kek and Keket, who were the first to leave Etelenty, went to Africa. The family of Heh and Hehet were the second to leave, and they went to Asia. The family of Nun and Nunit left next and went to Europe.

The family of Emen and Emenet were the last to leave Etelenty, and with them went the eight primordials, Tehuty, Ptah, and Khnemu. They went to Egypt (Kemit) on the northeast side of Africa and in the heart of the world. The eight primordials settled, with Tehuty, in the city called the City of Eight, Xemenu, or Net Tehuty (the City of Tehuty), which was later called Hermopolis, or the City of Hermes, by the Greeks. Ptah settled in Men-Nefer (Memphis) and Khnemu settled in Eunu (Heliopolis).

The emigration of the family of Emen and Emenet, along with the priesthood of Etelenty, took place in about 50,000 BCE. Upon settling in Egypt, they built the pyramids at Giza as the temple of initiation for the induction of new priests. Soon afterward, the five human principles were born, during the five intercalary days. These are the five days that are added to (intercalated) the 360-day solar year.

Out of the dark and mysterious water of Nu had come forth the divine pairing of Shu (air) and Tefnut (moisture). Together these entities brought forth Seb (earth) and Nut (heaven), who created the five human laws: on the first day came Oser (Osiris); on the second, Heru-Ur; on the third, Set; on the fourth, Est (Isis); and on the fifth, Nebt-Het (Nephthys). This concluded the creation of the nine Great Principles or Laws, or the Great Paut (the Enneagram), which is depicted as a nine-pointed star within a circle. These Great Laws of Eunu reflect all the qualities and dynamics that exist within the human psyche.

The Step Pyramid of Saqqara and its enclosure, which used to be the domain of the sages of ancient Egypt.

The Great Paut

In *The Book of the Dead*, we see the role of the nine great principles of Eunu (Heliopolis) in the life, death, and resurrection of the soul. The creator of the great company of nine laws in Eunu was the almighty God, Atum-Ra, described in Chapter 15 of *The Book of the Dead* as self-created, the maker of the laws of nature, creator of men, who stretched out heavens, who lights the Dwat (netherworld) with his two eyes (the Sun and Moon), and the creator of the north wind, which nourishes the souls of the dead.

1. Shu (air)

Shu is the first member of the company of laws in Eunu. He was created by God from the water of Nu as a twin with Tefnut. He is the personification of perfection, light, and the creator of air and space. Symbolically, he is depicted as a man (indicating masculinity), lifting up his arms and separating heaven from earth, which indicates the creation of space. He created the stairs, by which human beings can elevate themselves to reach heaven, and situated them in the City of Qaaemynu. He is the essence of the dry condition, masculine state, heat, light, and perfection.

2. Tefnut (moisture)

Tefnut is the second member of the Great Paut in Eunu. She is the twin sister of Shu and the personification of moisture. If Shu is the air, Tefnut is the moisture within air. She is the symbol of giving and generosity. She is depicted as a woman, with the head of a lioness, indicating power. Shu carries away hunger from the deceased, while Tefnut carries away their thirst.

The Djed colonnade, representing the evolution of mankind, and baboons, representing the spirits of dawn, all standing under heaven.

23

3. Seb (earth)

Seb is the third member of the Great Paut. His sacred bird is the goose. He is the offspring of Shu and Tefnut. Seb stimulates an individual's material world and provides them with a burial ground after death. Seb nourishes the human body upon earth and seals it for eternity in the tomb.

4. Nut (heaven)

Nut is the daughter of Shu and Tefnut and the domain of the stars and perfected souls. She is the emblem of romance, love, harmony, and the future of all souls. Heaven and earth (Seb and Nut) created the five human principles in Egypt, after the emigration from Etelenty. The dynamic action between these five principles established the qualities and traits of the human psyche.

5. Oser (Osiris)

Oser is the fifth member of the Great Paut of Eunu and the first son of heaven and earth. He was born on the first of the five intercalary days. Oser became the first king of Egypt and was the emblem of good, peace, and

The deceased receiving the water of immortal life from Nebt-Het, who is standing within the sycamore tree. A wall painting from the tomb of Kha, architect under Amenhotep III, New Kingdom, c. 15th/14th century BCE.

persuasion. He suffered terribly at the hands of his brother Set, and so he preferred to be the king of the afterlife, residing in the constellation of Orion in heaven, where the souls of the deceased came to rest after death, in the Fields of Earu or Garden of Reeds. The goal of the deceased was to unite with Oser, the emblem of good, in order to attain peace.

6. Heru-Ur (Horus the Great)

Heru-Ur, or Horus the Great, had similar qualities to a Heracles/Hercules of the Greeks. Heru-Ur is the emblem of power, strength, and conviction on all levels— physical, mental, and spiritual. The sphinx of Egypt, which is called Her-M-Akhety, or the light of the two horizons, is his model. The Egyptian sphinx has the body of a lion, which indicates physical strength, purification, and solar power. It has the neck of a bull, which implies spiritual purity and straightforwardness, and the head of a human, which implies divine intelligence, knowledge of good and evil, and the highest evolution of physical form. Heru-Ur played a significant role in the control, arrest, and judgment of evil. He subdued Set and brought him in chains to the Hall of Justice in Eunu (Heliopolis). He is the symbol of the Trooper, the avenger of the weak against the tyrant.

7. Set

Set was born on the third of the five intercalary days, at the wrong time and by the wrong means, forcing his way out of the womb. He became the instigator and founder

The Sphinx (Her-M-Akhety) standing before the pyramids as a guardian of sacred knowledge.

of evil on earth. He killed his brother Oser, the King of Egypt, and dismembered the body, cutting it into 14 pieces and scattering them all over Egypt. He is the emblem of indolence and rebellion. He committed countless acts of evil and became the symbol of the dark side of the human psyche. He was eventually defeated by Heru-Sheriu (Horus the Younger), the son of Est and Oser, and was arrested and subdued by Heru-Ur in the Great Hall of Justice.

8. Est (Isis)

Est was the wife of Oser, residing in heaven on Sirius (the Dog Star) at her husband's side. Oser resides in the Orion constellation. Est is the emblem of knowledge of medicine and magic, the mother of Heru, and the symbol of compassion and love. She is also the symbol of royal authority, having ruled Egypt, in Oser's absence, for 25 years. She is depicted in the form of a woman with a throne on her head.

9. Nebt-Het (Nephthys)

Nebt-Het is the ninth member of the Great Paut and the emblem of peace. She is the sister of Est and shared the suffering and grief of her sister. She is the mother of Enpu (Anubis) and the symbol of the time before sunrise. She is the instigator of prosperity and harmony in domestic life.

The temple of Isis at Philae, which was moved by the United Nations to an island on the River Nile.

27

Death and the Future of Departed Souls

The ancient Egyptian sages defined three worlds in which the soul dwells: Ta (earth), which is the typal world, or the world of appearances and material existence on earth; the Dwat (netherworld), which is the ectypal world, or the world of laws and shadows and the domain of the intermediate life of the soul in its journey through heaven; and finally, Nut (heaven), which is the archetypal world of forms and principles, and the learning ground and seed of all souls. These three worlds exist during the course of day and night. Ta (earth), the world of appearances, exists from 6 AM–6 PM. The Dwat, the world of laws and shadows, exists from 6 PM –midnight, and the heavenly kingdom exists from midnight–6 AM. We therefore experience all three worlds every day, coming forth during the day, then entering the Dwat and ascending to the heavenly domain. This was illustrated symbolically by two women stretching their arms and legs around the horizons, representing the day and night sky, while beneath them was Seb (earth), in a circular shape.

The Dwat exists within that circle of the body of earth. On the night an individual dies and enters the tomb, between 6 PM and midnight, his first resurrection and judgment occurs. This is illustrated in *The Book of the Dead* in the judgment scene, in which the deceased regains life in the tomb and stands before the 42 natural laws and Oser, the king of the afterlife. Tehuty is also

King Tut-Ankh-Emen (the living image of the hidden light) traveling in the underworld. He holds the scepter of authority in his left hand and the scepter of light in his right hand.

A golden shrine holding the canopic jars of King Tut, with a statue of Serqet,
the symbol of protection and guardianship, protecting the shrine.

present to record the works, deeds, and future of the soul of the deceased, while Enpu (Anubis) holds the scales of justice, upon which all the deeds of the deceased are weighed against the truth. All the bodily organs of the deceased become witnesses to his or her deeds. They become witnesses against the deceased if he or she denies any act committed in life. The deceased observes all the deeds he or she has done in his or her earthly life, in sound and sight, like watching a movie. The individual must then decide the fate of his or her future life, based on the deeds that were committed during the previous life.

Before human beings can acquire the supreme bliss of the higher heavens, they must overcome all the intermediary stages in their consciousness. If, during this life, the deceased have succeeded in identifying themselves and their organs with the laws of nature, further incarnations become unnecessary and they become one with the laws and free from the world of appearances. If the deceased have not acknowledged their own Ka (desire body), however, they will continue to return to earth many times.

Some principles mentioned in *The Book of the Dead* require an explanation:

Renutt (the law of harvest)

This is the law that turns the humors of a mother's blood into milk, and feeds the roots of trees and their fruits and the seeds buried in the ground. Through this law, the Djed of Oser, or the column of stability, is erected continually in nature.

Meskhent (the law of the birth chamber)

This is the law that makes hidden things appear, planted things rise, and causes children to be born.

Neserser (the island of fire)

This is the testing ground of souls as they travel through the underworld.

Rastau

This is part of the spiritual path of Sokar, the lord of death, judgment, and burial. There are two spiritual paths: northern and southern. The southern path (indirect) is the path of reincarnation, and the northern path (direct) is the path of immortality. Rastau is part of the northern path, and is the gateway and the center of the Dwat (netherworld). On earth, Rastau exists in the area of Saqqara, which is the domain of the sages.

The soul of the deceased travels the path to the Garden of Reeds, Sekhet-Earu, which is situated within the Field of Peace, Sekhet-Hetep. Sekhet-Earu is situated in heaven in the Orion constellation, while Sekhet-Hetep includes the constellations of Orion, Taurus, and Leo. The soul of the deceased then travels eastward to the Dog Star, Sirius, accompanied by the children of Heru (the spirits or energy in the stomach, liver, lungs, and intestine). These children of light are the companions of the soul of the deceased, and spiritually they form the Eb (spiritual heart), the Ka (desire body), and the Kha (spirit). The soul then travels northward to the Great Bear constellation, where it is purified by the Great Ennead (the nine principles) and the Lesser Ennead. This completes the course of the journey of a blessed soul who has accumulated a higher level of consciousness on earth.

I look forward to a true brotherhood in which we will not know separation from one another, even in death, since this unity would surpass the land of the dead and beyond. Only people with courage will make a difference in this life, not for glory but for true change in their flesh and bones. The human body is not manufactured to last for a few years; it is manufactured to last forever. This knowledge of eternity is available within *The Egyptian Book of the Dead*. It can provide solutions to the crisis faced by modern people.

The deceased making an offering of fruits to his own soul. This represents all the good deeds that he had cultivated in his own life. A fragment of a relief from the tomb of Sekeh, mayor of Memphis, New Kingdom, 18th dynasty.

The Versions of The Book of the Dead

The Book of the Dead was originally called *The Rescensions of Coming Forth by Day*, and is composed of four versions which represent four regions and four periods of time:

1. The Heliopolitan Version

This version was written in Medu-Netru (hieroglyphs). It was edited by the ancient priests of the college of Eunu (Heliopolis), based upon different texts, which are now lost. This version is known from five copies, which are inscribed upon the walls of the chambers and passages in pyramids of the kings of the 5th and 6th Dynasties at Saqqara. These pyramids are the Pyramids of Unes, Tete, Pepi I, Mentu-M-Sa-F, and Pepi II. They were excavated by Mariette and Maspero during 1880 and 1884, and the hieroglyphic texts from them, commonly known as the "Pyramid Texts," were published in Paris, with a French translation, between 1882 and 1893. In the 11th, 12th, and 13th Dynasties, many monuments were inscribed with sections of the texts of the Pyramid of Unes at Saqqara. For example, lines 206–269 are found, written in hieroglyphs, upon the coffin of Amamu (British Museum, No. 6654), lines 268–284 are

inscribed on the coffin of Epe Ankh, lines 268–289 on the coffin of Entef, line 206 on the coffin of Mentu-Hetep at Berlin, and lines 269–294 on the sarcophagus of Heru-Hetep. A section was found on the walls of the tomb of Queen Nefru, other sections were found on the sarcophagus of Dage, lines 5–8 occur on the stela of Epe, lines 166 onward were found on the Stela of Nehi, and lines 576–583 on the coffin of Sebek-Aa. In the 18th Dynasty, line 169 was copied onto a wall in the Temple of Queen Hatshepsut at Der-el-Bahri, and copies of lines 379–399 were found in the papyri of Mut-Hetep (British Museum, No. 10,010) and Nefer-Uten-F (Paris, No. 3092). In the 26th Dynasty, texts of the 5th Dynasty were repeated on the walls of the Tomb of Peta Emen Ept, the Chief of Kher-Heb at Thebes (Uast), and also upon the papyrus written for the Lady Sais in c. 200 CE. Some sections of this version were also found transcribed upon stelae, coffins, and papyrus books from the 11th Dynasty to c. 200 CE, as mentioned previously.

2. The Theban Version

This version was written in Medu-Netru (hieroglyphs). It was written upon papyrus books and was divided into sections, with specific titles. This version was used from the 18th to the 20th Dynasties.

3. The Generic Version Number One

This version was closely allied to the Theban version but was written on papyrus books in Medu-Netru and Hieratic (the abridged form of cursive hieroglyphic writing). The chapters in this version have no fixed order. They were used in the 20th Dynasty.

4. The Saite Version

This version was written in Medu-Netru and Hieratic. It was used from the 26th Dynasty up to the end of the Ptolemaic period. The chapters of this version were arranged in a definite order.

Lepsius, in his edition of the Turin Papyrus published in 1842, divided *The Book of the Dead* into the well-known chapters that we have today. However, this division is inaccurate, has no titles, and the chapters do not relate to one another.

A Bedouin contemplates the Step Pyramid at Saqqara.

— 2 —

THE SYMBOLISM OF THE EGYPTIAN MEDU-NETRU

The word "language" is derived from the Latin lingua, which means "the tongue," and "age" and therefore means "the speech of ages." The Egyptian words for language are Ddt, Medu, or Ra-N-Kemit. The root of the word Ddt is the verb Dd, which means "to say," "speak," or "declare." The utterance of sound is energy resonating in spiral form, which is represented by the snake, the symbol of primordial energy, while the hand expresses the use of this sound resonation in communication. The Medu-Netru is the symbolic writing of the Ancient Egyptians, which is usually known as hieroglyphs.

THE ORIGINS OF LANGUAGE

The original language of mankind was founded in Atlantis by Tehuty (Hermes). His name, therefore, is usually written starting with the snake, although sometimes it starts with the hand. Tehuty chose a language that would always remind the user of nature and its laws. This language, the Medu-Netru, is composed of all of nature, whether made by God or man, and its origin was a divine revelation, which embodied the word of God or the natural laws (the "logos" of the Greeks).

The first inhabitants of the British Isles kept the original language of Atlantis alive, using symbols of trees, flowers, and animals. Initially, they only used ten main symbols in their language, but later Beli Mawr (the Great), the Celtic God of the Sun, added another six symbols, calling these 16 symbols "letter signs" or "Ystorrynau." It was the Britain Gwydion that introduced the 16 letter signs to Greece, thereby supplying the Greeks with their Kadmus.

The Nile crocodile is a symbol of time in the Egyptian language.

The Medu-Netru is sacred. It uses symbols, not letters. A symbol exists in nature and has a geometrical value, volume, sound, energy, and effect, while a letter is merely an intellectual line drawing. This language, therefore, connects the individual with reality and the laws governing it in a direct way. When you write the word "crocodile" in Egyptian, you actually draw the crocodile itself. This puts you in direct contact with the crocodile as a living creature—more so, because the crocodile's biological functions reflect the natural laws governing this creature. The female crocodile, for example, has bird-like qualities since it lays eggs, and its heart and kidneys are similar to those of birds, but its lungs are those of a mammal. The crocodile, therefore, reflects duality in nature, and so the ancient Egyptian temples dedicated to the crocodile principle had two sanctuaries, as in the temple of Kom Ombo.

The crocodile is also like a fish, in that it spends the night in water, but like a mammal since it spends the day on land. This implies that the crocodile is a solar animal and is connected with the sun, emerging from the water when the sun rises on the horizon and disappearing into the water when the sun sets.

The female crocodile carries its eggs for sixty days and broods on them for sixty days. It has sixty vertebrae and sixty teeth, and lives for sixty years. Number sixty is the basic unit in astronomy and the measurement of time, since the minute is sixty seconds and the hour is sixty minutes. The crocodile, therefore, reflects the principle of time, and in the Egyptian word *Sebek*, meaning crocodile, the syllable, *Seb*, means time.

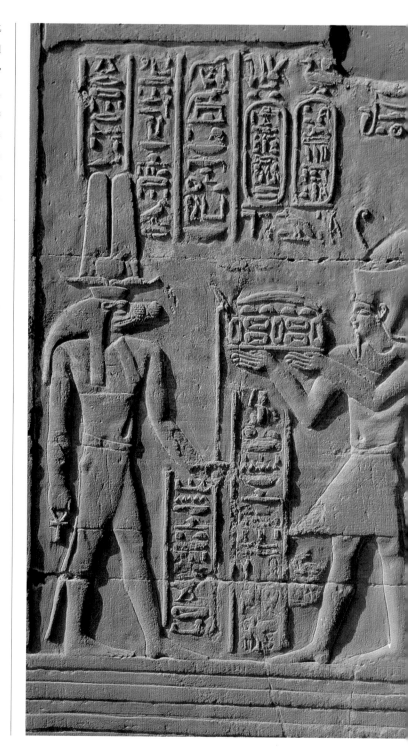

The King of Egypt making an offering to the crocodile principle (Sebek) as a symbol of the balance and justice of his earthly deeds.

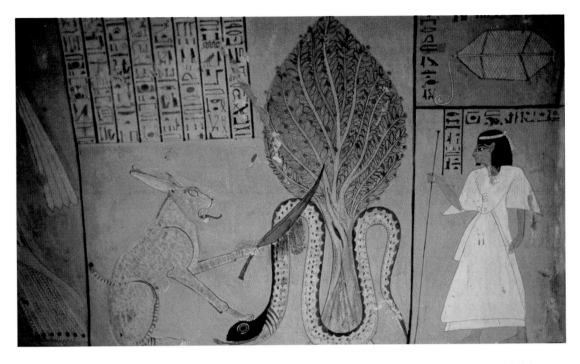

The sacred cat (Bast) under the sycamore tree of Eunu (Heliopolis), cutting the serpent of darkness as a symbol of the victory of light over darkness and knowledge over ignorance. A mural from the tomb of Sennedjem.

The crocodile also expresses our understanding of earthly time as action through duality. It possesses strong eyesight, which expresses the power of initiative, and it sees only forward and sideways, not backward, emphasizing the idea of time, since it is only possible for time to travel forward.

Thus it was that Tehuty, the founder of all human knowledge, employed natural symbols and images to represent the elementary powers, and express the ectypal and archetypal forms of existence. We can gain a similar insight into this natural world by reading *Aesop's Fables* or the *Conference of the Birds*, where animals are used as a means of expressing actions that have no material carriers. This quality is missing from our modern, conventional languages, which use cursive writing.

The following are some examples of the vast array of symbols that are used within the Egyptian language and its complex mythology:

The snake, Epep, in the Egyptian mythology was originally an enormous water reptile.

The water cow represents earth and the earthly path, as depicted in the cow couch in Egyptian mythology.

The twins Shu (dry) and Tefnut (moisture) were represented as a lion and lioness.

The virgin woman was expressed by a female vulture, since it was believed that the female vulture became pregnant merely by exposing herself to the wind.

The provider was represented by a goose.

The leader or king was represented by a honey bee. The word for a honey bee was *Bt*, which was also the word for honey itself, and symbolizes the substance of the soul. The soul was called *Ba*, from which the English word "bee" is derived.

The artist was represented by a scarab, since it is in a continuous state of regeneration.

The physician was represented by an ibis bird, since it administered enemas to itself.

The judge was represented by a mouse, since it eats the best part of the bread. It was also represented by a jackal because it hides its food in earth until it has putrefied and then brings it out to eat. Another symbol for the judge was the baboon (cynocephalus), since it cries in the absence of the moon (light), and rejoices and sings when the moon (light) emerges. The wig used in the British courts of law today is a representation of the wig of the baboon.

The mystic initiate was represented by a grasshopper or mantis, since the insect does not emit any sound from its mouth but makes a chirping sound using its spinal cord. This indicates that it is committed to the roots of life and that the divine needs no sound to express itself. The mantis was also a symbol of a leaper or dancer, and of the moon, which leaps to a new location every night. It also represents the initiate, leaping into the light.

The frog, Heqat, represented the seer or foreteller of events, since it predicted the inundation of the Nile. Its transformation from a tadpole, without legs, to a frog represents the initiate who reaches immortality. Lamps in ancient Egypt used to have a frog over them as a symbol of the rising sun. Ptah, the first craftsman on earth, was also symbolized by a frog-headed man as a symbol of the creative power overcoming matter.

Animals were given their names according to the original sound that they uttered. The goose, for example, utters a hissing sound, and so it was given the name *Sa*. The ram and goat were given the name *Ba* because that is the sound they make. The hippopotamus was given the name *Reret*, because of its roaring sound, while the lion's roar gave it the name *Ru*. The ibis bird utters the sound "Eaah," and therefore *Eaah* became one of its names. This is also the word for the moon, since the ibis represents the moon.

The horned viper was chosen to express the sound "F" in the alphabet because of the puffing sound that it makes, using the power of breath, and even today the letter "F" in the English alphabet still contains the two horns of the viper. If you turn the letter "F" sideways, it resembles the horned viper.

A jewelled pectoral with a scarab adorning the center. These were often worn as protective amulets.

One of the capstones which were used to balance
the energy in the area of Eunu (Heliopolis).

The light of the Sun, or the giver of life, is symbolized by a circle, in the center of which is a point of polarization. The circle represents God, since it has no beginning, no end, and no middle, while the center represents the point of polarization, which is God's idea or thought to create.

Light is one of the two main elements of creation, the other being sound. These are the only two absolute phenomena in nature; everything else is relative. The light and rays of the Sun (the giver of life) embody the spirits of the souls who made a conscious choice at the beginning of creation to remain in the original state of happiness, close to God. This light, without which life would cease to exist, is called *Ra*, and is composed of the mouth, which is a symbol for divine reason and the sacred sound that created the universe, and the forearm, which is the symbol for strength and the power of action. The word Ra, therefore, clearly explains the nature of light, which exists by divine reason and gives life through the strength of the original cause (the original state of happiness). Other words derived from this symbol give further indications of the nature of both sound and light, such as "illumination," "to illumine," "diet," "light," "light of lights," or "day," "time," etc.

The symbol for the constellation of Orion is Saah, whose root is based on the three constellations that conduct the process of reincarnation and the transmigration of the soul. This symbol consists of three loops on top of a phallus (the age-old symbol of regeneration), which represent the constellations of Taurus, Leo, and Orion.

Other symbols used to express the same concept and carrying the same sound value are founded upon the phallus (regeneration), but the first replaces the loops with two symbols for bones, while the other has two axes, the symbol for a law or principle. The two symbols represent Oser (Osiris), who is the king of the Dwat (netherworld), and Heru, who is the guide for the blessed souls in the kingdom of heaven, and resides in the constellation of Leo. The lost and wicked souls are ruled by Set (Satan), who resides in the constellation of Taurus. All the words derived from this symbol indicate the nature of Oser and Heru, who guide and open doors for the blessed souls in the netherworld. The word *Saahsaah*, for instance, means "to approach," although

Egyptologists have mistranslated these symbols as "toes" or "legs" because of the word *Saaht*, which means "legs" or "feet." Orion was called "the leg of heaven" by the ancient Egyptians.

The chick is the symbol of innocence and simplicity.

The Ankh (a looped cross) is the symbol of life, since it includes within itself the three elementary powers of creation: Emen-Ra, the sound which caused creation, Reh, and the water of Nu (water of chaos).

The Djed is the symbol of stability and good foundation since it represents the spinal column of Oser and the four elementary systems in the human body (the skeletal system, the muscular system, the blood circulation system, and the nervous systems).

The Uast is the symbol of power and authority of action, since it represents the idea of crossing.

The linen fold represents the power of action and execution because the members of the Egyptian senate used to carry a linen fold over their arm to indicate their position. This later changed to be a golden pin, worn on the collar, indicating a man or woman of action, and so this symbol became the emblem of health and happiness, as in the word *Senb* (health).

The Cartouche is called *Shen*, meaning that which is encircled by the sun will always be eternal.

According to the ancient Egyptian doctrine of metempsychosis, the soul of the deceased passes through the underworld, transforming into different forms of animals, reptiles, insects, and birds. This process of metamorphosis has been interpreted and represented in a different way by the Indian and Greek traditions.

Of royal descent, Thutmose I holds a double Ankh in both hands as a symbol of life here and life hereafter.

With some exceptions, insects, or *Haiu*, were considered symbolic of the lower grades of incarnated souls. Locusts, for example, were considered emblematic of destruction, ruin, disease, hate, strife, and passion. Butterflies, which are seen to emerge from a chrysalis, were the symbol of metamorphosis. Ants were symbols of industry and foresight, since they store food in summer for the winter and are capable of moving objects many times their own weight. They also were symbols for initiates, since ants manage to find what man has hidden, like initiates who seek to find knowledge that has been hidden. Indeed, the Egyptian initiates were divided into three different grades, according to their evolution:

Scarabs, or *Khepru*, which reflect light, truth, and regeneration.

Lions, or *Ru*, which reflect guardianship, strength, power of vision, and purification.

Leopards, or *Abu*, which reflect mystery and the unknown.

Scorpions were symbols of guardians, since Est (Isis) assigned seven scorpions for her protection. They were also a symbol of the accused because the rulership of Set (Satan) and the death of Oser (Osiris) took place when the Sun entered the sign of Scorpio.

In the Egyptian mythology, the body of Oser, the first king of Egypt, was dismembered and the pieces dispersed throughout Egypt by his brother, Set. This

42

A row of ram-headed sphinxes before the temple of Emen at Karnak, representing the sacrifices of the human soul.

dismemberment represents disorder, which scatters divinity. The incident called for harmony and, by the law of affinity, the scattered parts of Oser (divinity) come together. Thus, a new light emerged out of darkness and order out of disorder.

The moment, hour, day, month, year, and the movements of the stars contain the rhythms of atoms, cells, and all that exists. The process of gestation involves destruction and building, as, for example, in human cells, which are destroyed and renewed every day. During the evolution of man and the souls of all living things, the causal energy becomes mineral, mineral becomes vegetable, vegetable becomes animal, animal becomes man, and man becomes superman (i.e. the sage or immortal—see the commentary on the Doctrine of Longevity). The underlying quality of this evolution, however, is suffering, due to the original decision of all embodied souls to leave the Creator. The minerals, therefore, suffer separation from the original cause (the original state of happiness), plants suffer the minerals' lives, animals suffer plants' lives, man suffers animals' lives, and supermen suffer humanity. This suffering is, in reality, consciousness undergoing the process of transforming itself.

Before human beings can acquire the supreme bliss of higher heavens, they must transcend all intermediary stages in their consciousness. If, during this lifetime, they succeed in identifying themselves and their organs with the laws of nature, further incarnations are no longer necessary and they become one with the laws, and therefore free from the world of appearances.

If, on the other hand, an individual's experience during this lifetime remains incomplete, they will have to wait in the field of offerings and then return to earth. However, a human being who has not acknowledged their Ka (inner nature) may only return to earth five times, and so we find many references within *The Book of the Dead* to the aspiration of the deceased to unite with the natural laws.

The fact that the Egyptian language uses symbols and not letters means that it cannot be translated in the way that we translate English or French, for instance. Consider this example. Human beings have two eyes, which are considered as one of the four gates of the human soul. The verb "to see," therefore, is written with the two eyes, pronounced as "Maa." The word "insight," however, is written with the two eyes followed by a sickle, which is the shape of the bone in the middle of the skull that divides the brain into two halves. Images are seen first as dual and upside-down, but in the brain they become one. The right eye represents the Sun, which reflects the light of nature, while the left eye represents the Moon and the Oserian Ka. When people unite themselves with their higher Ka, their vision

The king of Egypt as a symbol of light and life, traveling through the sky as an evolved soul. A mural from the tomb of Thutmose III, Valley of the Kings.

Tehuty, the founder of human knowledge, in a kneeling position, holding the right eye which represents the light of the sun and knowledge.

becomes the vision of Maat (truth), which gives birth to the Horian eye, or what is called the third eye. When they start to see with their third eye, they become one with the laws of nature and can then rule their own destiny. The shape of the eye is an ellipse, which means "that which falls short of being perfectly round," i.e. a circle. This implies that the outer vision will always fall short of being perfect; only the inner vision can achieve this level of perfection.

A sentence, therefore, which says, *"I have eaten with my mouth and chewed with my jaws,"* does not express its true meaning in this literal translation. The symbolic meaning of eating with the mouth is that one digests what one eats; the symbolic meaning of chewing with the jaws is that one comprehends what one learns. The true translation of this text, therefore, should be, *"I digest what I learn and absorb what I comprehend."*

In Plate 9 of the Papyrus of Hunefer, it says:

If we try to translate this sentence literally, without consideration of the symbolic meaning, it would read:

"I am pure in my great double nests, in the city of Sutnny, in the day where the people gave offerings to the great principle in it."

However, this translation misses the meaning completely. If we look at the same sentence and consider its symbolic meaning, we will obtain the following translation:

"I achieved purification of my body and soul in the time of my youth, when other people were busy with the dazzling illusion of life."

The translations in this book incorporate the symbolic meaning of the texts.

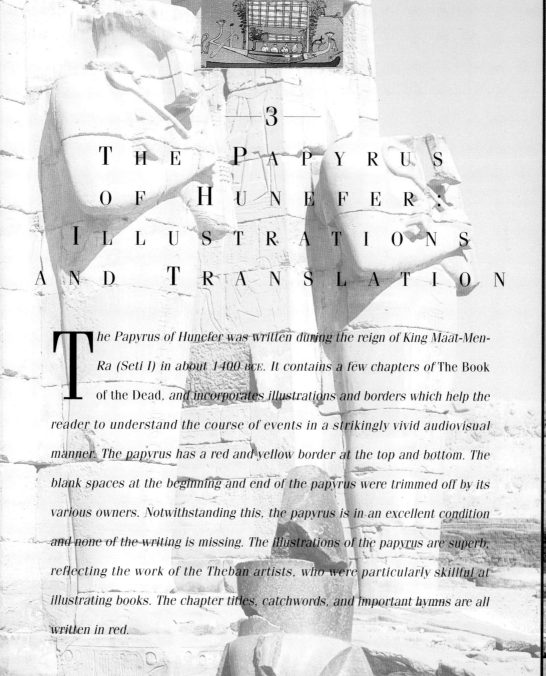

3
THE PAPYRUS
OF HUNEFER:
ILLUSTRATIONS
AND TRANSLATION

The Papyrus of Hunefer was written during the reign of King Maat-Men-Ra (Seti I) in about 1400 BCE. It contains a few chapters of The Book of the Dead, and incorporates illustrations and borders which help the reader to understand the course of events in a strikingly vivid audiovisual manner. The papyrus has a red and yellow border at the top and bottom. The blank spaces at the beginning and end of the papyrus were trimmed off by its various owners. Notwithstanding this, the papyrus is in an excellent condition and none of the writing is missing. The illustrations of the papyrus are superb, reflecting the work of the Theban artists, who were particularly skillful at illustrating books. The chapter titles, catchwords, and important hymns are all written in red.

Hunefer in Life

Hunefer acted in the capacity of the royal scribe and accountant of King Maat-Men-Ra (Seti I). He is described as the overseer of the palace of King Maat-Men-Ra, the royal scribe of his divine offering, the overseer of his cattle, and the governor of the west side of Uast (Thebes). Hunefer was married to a priestess of the Temple of Emen-Ra in Uast, whose name was Nasha. Nasha is depicted standing near to her husband, indicating the couple's closeness and support of one another's cause in life, since they were both committed members of the priesthood of Emen-Ra.

The text of the papyrus includes:

1 A hymn to the rising sun.

2 The declaration of Tehuty and an account of what he has done for Oser (Osiris), the principle of good.

3 The judgment of the deceased, with an illustration of the scene of weighing the deceased's deeds.

4 Chapters 1, 22, and 17 of *The Book of the Dead.*

5 Chapter of opening the mouth of Oser.

Hunefer's papyrus is considered to be the shortest text of *The Book of the Dead* of the Theban period.

P L A T E   I

CLOT BEY
9901

Illustration 1

Hunefer is depicted with his wife, Nasha, standing behind him in an adoration pose, at the entrance to the unknown. They are both wearing white linen, a symbol of purity. A priestly rosary hangs from Hunefer's left arm, while Nasha holds in her left hand the sistrum (a musical instrument), a symbol of resisting the power of evil in life, and the lotus flower, a symbol of life-giving. Another lotus flower is depicted above her head, representing Nasha's life-giving

quality as a woman. In front of Hunefer, a line of text is written, indicating his name and occupation:

"Beloved of Oser, overseer of the palace of the king, the master of the two lands (Egypt), Maat-Men-Ra (Seti I), overseer of the cattle of the master of the two lands and the royal scribe, Hunefer. May he be victorious as the governor of the west side of Uast (Thebes)." Above Nasha's image is written: *"Mistress, priestess of Emen, Nasha"*.

Illustration 2

Here, a falcon is depicted with a sun disk over his head and a cobra encircling the sun. This is the symbol of Mars, the guardian star, which appears on the horizon at both dawn and sunset. The name of Mars is Ra-Heru-Akhety, or the light of the two horizons. Four baboons are depicted in front of the symbol of Mars, in adoration pose, and there are three baboons behind, in the same posture. These seven baboons together represent the seven spirits of dawn, who evoke the seven powers in nature every day. The Djed is depicted below the falcon, representing the spinal column of Oser (Osiris), the four elementary systems of the human body (the skeletal, muscular, cardiovascular, and nervous systems), the four winds, the four cardinal points, and the four main organs, which are called the sons or children of Heru (the lungs, stomach, intestine, and liver). Two arms appear from the Djed. The right arm holds the Nekhekh scepter, the symbol of the North and strength, while the left arm holds the Heqa, the emblem of the South and the symbol of rulership. Est (Isis), Oser's wife, stands on the right side of the Djed and Nebt-Het (Nephthys), Est's sister, stands on the left. In front of the falcon, Ra-Heru-Akhety, a line of text is written: *"The spirits of dawn adore you, O light of the two horizons."* Behind the falcon is written: *"Adoration to the light of God, when it rises over the horizon."* In front of Est is written: *"I am your sister, Est, the divine mother."* In front of Nebt-Het is written: *"I am your sister, Nebt-Het."*

PLATE 1

Egypt at dawn—a view from Mount Sinai.

Translation

1 *Adoration to the light of God in nature, when it rises on the horizon in the eastern side of heaven.* **2** *Behold Hunefer, who is united with Oser, victoriously! He said, "Homage to you, the principle of light, in his rising and setting.* **3** *You rise (repeat this twice), you shine (repeat this twice), glorious as the king of the laws.* **4** *You are the lord of heaven and earth, maker of the heavenly beings above and the beings below, one principle, who came into being, maker of the world, creator of mankind, maker of the water of Nu, creator of the river Nile, maker of the water which gives life therein, binding the mountains, causing the existence of humanity and cattle. Maker of heaven and earth, adoration to you!* **5** *O, you are embraced by Maat at the two seasons. You are striding over heaven with joy.* **6** *The evil one has fallen and his two arms are cut off. The Sektet boat receives the beautiful winds and the heart of the one who dwells in his shrine is glad.* **7** *You are crowned as the leader of heaven. You are the one who is provided with everything and the light of the truth comes from the cosmic ocean of Nu with victory.* **8** *O divine youth, heir of eternity, self-begotten, giving birth to himself, mighty one of the multitude of forms, king of the two lands, ruler of Eunu, lord of eternity, and ruler of everlasting things.* **9** *The company of the nine principles (Paut) rejoices, when your light rises.* **10** *You sail across the horizon and you are exalted in the Sektet boat. Homage to you, hidden light of the truth. You sail across the sky and cause the existence of everyone who looks at you.* **11** *Your majesty* *grows and strides and your beams of light shine upon all faces.* **12** *You are unknown and no tongue can claim that there is another one but you. You are the one who brings life to the chamber of growth.* **13** *Men worship you in your name; they swear by you for you are lord over them.* **14** *You listen with your ears and see with your eyes.* **15** *Millions of years have passed over the world and I cannot count the number of years which have passed by you. Your heart has decreed a day of happiness in your name of traveler. You have journeyed over rivers of millions and hundreds of thousands of millions of years. You sail over them in peace and steer your way over the watery abyss, which is the place that you love.* **16** *You do all of this in a short hour of time. You sit in peace and cause the end of hours. Behold! Beloved of Oser, the overseer of the royal house of the master of the two lands, Hunefer, victorious, said: 'Hail, my lord, who passes through eternity and whose existence is everlasting!* **17** *Hail, the disk of the Sun, the lord of rays, who causes everything to live! Grant that the scribe, Hunefer, who is united with Oser, may see you at dawn time every day.'"*

The Hathor temple of Queen Nefertari at Abu Simbel, built by Ramses II. It was moved from Nubia to its present location by the United Nations.

PLATE 1

Commentary

This introduction to the Book of Hunefer in Plate 1 is ceremonial and takes the form of a hymn of praise to the one, almighty God, who created everything. It refutes the misconception commonly held by modern Egyptologists that the Egyptians were polytheistic, although the pioneers of Egyptology, such as Champollion, Maspero, and others, did recognize that the Egyptians embraced only one God. Many of today's Egyptologists have been influenced by the religions of Judaism, Christianity, and Islam, which in general maintain that the ancient Egyptians were heathen and polytheistic, a view that arises from a lack of understanding of the Egyptian spiritual doctrines. It is, therefore, all the more ironic to consider that the founders of Judaism and Christianity were themselves educated in Egypt, although their own people did not share their views during their lifetime. Moses, for example, became lost alone in the desert of Sinai, while Jesus was crucified by the very people who later glorified him. In the midst of this ignorance, the views that were held about the Egyptians became distorted.

The ancient Egyptians, in reality, had one of the most advanced spiritual systems in the history of humanity, and it is important to understand the basis of this spiritual

system in order to be able to comprehend their elaborate culture. The spiritual doctrines of ancient Egypt include the doctrine of faith, which is the foundation of everything in this life. The question that someone might raise is "faith in what?" The answer is faith in the one almighty Creator, who created everything by the exercise of his own will. As Tehuty (Hermes), the founder of this spiritual system and the original author of *The Book of the Dead*, said: "*None of our thoughts are capable of conceiving God, nor any language of defining Him. That which is incorporeal, formless, invisible cannot be grasped by our senses. That which is eternal cannot be measured by the short rules of time. God is, accordingly, ineffable.*"

The names that are given to God by mankind are merely an expression of their understanding of God. The ancient Egyptians called God "Atum-Ra," where "Atum" means "the beginning," or "the source," and also means "the end," while "Ra" means "light." The name Atum-Ra, therefore, means the beginning and end of all light. Another of the Egyptian names for God was "Emen-Ra," where "Emen" means "hidden" or "invisible." Emen-Ra, therefore, means the hidden light. God was also known as "Eaau," where "Ea" means "polarization" and "Au" means "expansion." The word "Eaau," therefore, indicates the meaning of the power that was polarized and expanded, creating the universe.

All creations came forth in the far beginning by the power of faith. God is, in truth, an eternal presence, and God is closer to each living person than the aorta in his or her own heart.

The entrance to the colonnade hall
in the temple of Karnak.

In *The Book of the Dead*, it says: "*These are the words of the master of all limits: 'I became the creator of what came into being. I came into being like the form of the sunrise, coming into being in the beginning of time.'*"

Faith compels the living human toward conviction and unshakable beliefs, and the ancient Egyptians, therefore, valued life in its eternity. They built temples, which became the objects of eternity and everlasting principles. The temples are still very much alive and yet, while the messages recorded in their stones live for eternity, not a single house of any of the Egyptian kings survived because the king's house, which was called the White House, was built out of mud bricks and had to be built anew for every king. This indicates their belief that the house of the king expressed the mortal and secular side of life, while the house of God (the temple) was representative of the eternal and everlasting.

God, according to the ancient Egyptians, is the first, incorruptible, eternal, unmade, indivisible, and incomparable, the author of all good, the wisest of the wise, the father of justice, self-taught, and absolutely perfect. God is the parent of the world, the builder of the soul, and the maker of both heaven and earth. He cannot be known by reason and, if he is known, it is impossible to explain this knowledge in words. God makes himself present through the whole world but particularly in the center, which is the heart of the just.

The text in Plate 1 incorporates a song of praise to the Creator as the cause and origin of all creations and His light, which comes to earth through the Sun. This light gives life to everything in our world, and the text, therefore, speaks of the light of God in nature (the Sun) as "embraced by Maat at the two seasons." Maat means the truth and the two seasons are life here and life hereafter, implying that light is unchangeable and everlasting. It also refers to the Sun "striding over heaven with joy," meaning that it causes our time on earth. The Sektet boat refers to the journey of the sunlight between the hours of noon to midnight, and the text speaks of the sunlight causing wind and the generation of air, which gives life to every living human, and particularly to the human who values the sacredness of life.

The Creator is described as the one who brings life into the womb ("chamber of growth"). He is also described as listening with His ears (meaning day and night), and seeing with His eyes (meaning the Sun and Moon), since it is through day and night that we perceive the concepts of good and evil. If there were no day, we would not know the meaning of night, and vice versa, and it is through the Sun and Moon that we are governed by earthly time, causing the duration of our organs in this lifetime. The Sun and Moon are the two eyes of God, through which He looks at us.

The text also indicates that God has "decreed a day of happiness" through the power of sound, which causes everything to exist and maintains this existence, adding that the origin and time limit of God's existence is unknown and that God exists within the ocean of harmony. The universe, according to the ancient sages, is composed of 183 worlds. It is formed in the shape of an equilateral triangle, on each dimension of which there are 60 worlds, with one world in each angle of the triangle. In the middle of the triangle exists the Plane of Truth, which is the essence of the universal harmony.

The text draws to a conclusion with God causing the life and death of every creature and accomplishing all of this in no more than a moment of time. It therefore ends with a request that Hunefer may be given eternal life by embracing the rays of the Sun.

PLATE 2

Illustration 1

Hunefer is depicted with his wife standing behind him, in adoration pose. In front of Hunefer is written: *"Beloved of Oser, overseer of the cattle of the king, Maat-Men-Ra, master of the two lands, scribe of divine offerings, overseer of the house of the king, Hunefer, governor of the west side of Uast."*

Illustration 2

Tehuty is standing, holding in his left hand the symbol of the mastery of life and the authority of knowledge.

Translation

1 *Adoration to Oser! Let praises be given to him and homage and prostration before the master of the Red Land! I exalt those who wander over his land. Behold, beloved of Oser, overseer of the house of the King of the two lands.* **2** *Hunefer, who is victorious, said: "I come to you, son of Nut, Oser, ruler of eternity. I am one of the followers of Tehuty; I rejoice at all that he has done.* **3** *He brought you the sweet winds for your nostrils to give you life and he brought the beautiful wind to your face, which comes forth from Tumu for your nose, O master of the*

PLATE 2

Red Land. **4** He granted that Shu (principle of air) shine over your body. **5** He illumined the way for you with light. **6** He forgave you the sins of your body, by the glory of his utterance. **7** He pacified the two Herus (Heru-Ur [Hercules] and Heru-Sheriu [Horus the Younger]) as two brothers. **8** He destroyed storms and whirlwinds for you. **9** He caused the two fighters (Heru and Set) to be gracious to you. **10** For you, he destroyed the shame in their hearts. He reconciled them and made your son, Heru, victorious in the presence of the company of the nine laws (Paut), giving him complete sovereignty over earth and letting him rule over all of it. **11** He granted him the throne of Seb (earth) in excellence, which was found by Tumu, and established this by decree in the archive chamber, inscribing it on a slab of iron, in accordance with the command of your father, Ptahtanen, upon the great throne. **12** He granted that his brother (Oser) should preside over that which supports Shu (air), to stretch out the water over the mountains and to make things grow on earth. **13** He granted providence by water and earth. **14** For your son, Heru, he decreed that the laws of heaven and earth **15** should follow him to his chamber, observe his commands, and execute them straight away. **16** Your heart is glad, O master of all the gracious laws. Egypt, the Red Land, is in peace and the laws uphold your dominion. **17** Temples are established in their locations, cities, and nomes (states). **18** Behold their names; we will pay our respects to you in divine offerings and make sacrifices in your name forever. **19** We call out to you in praise of your name, pouring water for your Ka, and funeral offerings are brought forth by all good souls, who are in your fellowship. The divine company of the nine laws (Paut) pours life-giving water on both sides of this land for all the departed souls that live in it. **20** They fulfilled your plans, all according to God's orders, at the beginning of time. You are, therefore, crowned as the son of Nut (heaven), even as the master of all limits in his rising. **21** Your living is established and you are becoming youthful with the truth. **22** Your Father, Ra (light), preserves you. **23** The nine laws give praises to you. **24** Est is with you and she cannot be separated

Sculptured pillars line a corridor which leads to the central chamber of the larger of two sandstone temples to Ramses II at Abu Simbel.

The Nile continues to be a valuable source of water to those living in Egypt today. Here, women collect water in large water jugs to transport back to their families.

from you. Your enemies cannot overthrow you. The masters of the world praise your beauty as they do the light of God in nature, when it rises at dawn. **25** You rise in height, upon your standard; your beauty exalts the face and broadens the step. **26** You are given the sovereignty of your father, Seb (earth), who created your beauty. **27** Your mother transforms you; heaven, who gave birth to the laws of nature, gave birth to you as the greatest of the five human principles. **28** You are established as the King and you wear the white crown on your head. **29** You grasped the crook and the flail. **30** You were crowned as the lord of the two lands, even while you were in your mother's womb. The Atef crown of light was upon your forehead. All the laws came to you, bowing before you, and, out of respect, they trace their steps backward."

PLATE 2

Commentary

The text in Plate 2 is a hymn of praise to Oser (Osiris). Oser was the eldest of the five human principles and became the first king of Egypt, embracing the virtue and conviction of good. He ruled for 28 years, 25 of which he spent outside Egypt, speaking to the rest of mankind about justice, faith, and virtue. He did not bring an army with him in his travels, but was accompanied by priests, musicians, and singers. He trusted in the power of persuasion and harmony, in the conviction that we are here to develop good rather than to fight evil. He taught mankind the art of agriculture, encouraging the cultivation of fruit and vegetables, in preference to cannibalism.

Oser was born on the first of the five intercalary days, which is equivalent to July 15th in our modern calendar. The creation of the five human principles was a cosmic event, observed by the immortals of Etelenty and the beings of light, who stood in the golden light of the rising Sun, dressed in fine, white linen, and sang a morning song, which awakened even the dead. Baboons raised their hands to heaven, scorpions stood still, chicks burst out of their eggs, cattle became pregnant, fish leapt with joy in the water of the Nile, and fig trees grew heavy with fruit, palm trees with dates, and vines with dark-purple grapes. Barley and wheat sprang up and the Nile flooded with green water from far south, rendering Egypt's land fertile. Oser was given authority over the water of the Nile and its banks, which facilitate life for all. His name means the vision of authority.

Oser's absence from Egypt gave his brother, Set (Satan), 25 years in which to hatch a plot against him, with the help of 72 conspirators, including Aso, the Queen of Ethiopia. Set constructed a chest of cedarwood in the shape of a man, with the exact measurements of Oser, who was a little more than 5 m. 14 cm. tall. The chest was inlaid with golden leaves and a thousand gems of carnelian and turquoise. On its lid, Oser's face was depicted in black, shining ebony, with lips of carnelian and eyes of bright lapis lazuli and ivory. On the side of the chest was a portrait of Nut (heaven), with a deep blue body and a belly spangled with yellow stars. Queen Aso of Ethiopia laid her charms of eternity, sleep, and binding over the chest.

On Oser's return, Set held a banquet for him in the city of Abdu (Abydos). Oser embraced his brother and kissed him on the cheeks, glad that Set had forgotten their differences. Set brought his gift, wrapped in white linen, and offered it to whoever could lie in it and fit it exactly. Everyone cheered, and one by one tried to fit into the chest, but it was too large for them. They persuaded Oser to try his luck, and eventually he relented and lay down in the chest. The conspirators slammed the lid shut on him and nailed the lid down with iron nails, filling the cracks between the lid and the box with melted lead. Some of the guests tried to save Oser, but they were too weak to lift the lid, which was heavily inlaid with jewels and metals. The conspirators hacked at them with their swords and spears, and the rest of the guests ran away.

Set and the 72 conspirators carried the chest to the river and threw it into the Nile. Set stood over it, saying: *"He drowns in his own waters. He is trapped in form, inert. He is cut down like his own stalks of wheat. Ever after, his name shall be 'Still heart, ruler of the land of the Dead.'"* With a cry of victory, Set ran back to the palace, where he drank Oser's drink, ate his honeyed cakes, and ordered about and beat his brother's servants. Then he fell asleep in the soft, perfumed sheets of his brother's bed.

The chest drifted to the waters of the Mediterranean and finally to the beach of Byblos, where a huge Erica tree grew around the chest, enclosing it in its trunk. The King of Byblos ordered the tree to be cut down and erected as a colonnade in his palace.

Meanwhile, Est, Oser's wife, had set out in search of her husband's body. Arriving at Byblos, she disguised herself as a maid in the royal palace of Byblos. She soon revealed her identity, however, and persuaded the King and Queen to cut the trunk of the tree open and give her back the chest, which contained Oser's body. On her return to Egypt, she hid the chest in the papyrus marshes and visited it every day, putting magic charms over Oser's body until he came back to life. She also raised her son, Heru, in the papyrus marshes, hiding him from his evil uncle, but Set eventually discovered the hideaway when he was hunting one night in the moonlight. While Oser was embracing Heru, Set stabbed Oser with his obsidian knife and hacked him into 14 pieces. He gave each piece to one of his conspirators, in order to apportion the feeling of guilt among them and enforce the support of his rulership.

Est again traveled all over Egypt, sailing on the Nile marshes in a papyrus boat, in order to collect the scattered remains of her husband's body. She erected a shrine over each of the pieces.

Meanwhile, Heru-Sheriu (Horus the Younger), the son of Oser and Est, was ready to reclaim his father's throne and waged three battles against Set. In the first one, Heru was victorious. He castrated Set and put him in Est's custody, but she pitied him and set him free. Two other battles followed, in which Heru was again victorious. In the second one, the 42 natural laws helped him to restore the throne of Egypt and, with Tehuty's assistance, Heru was able to establish good rulership once more throughout the land.

However, when the battle recommenced and began to involve all of nature, including animals, God ordered that the battle must stop and harmony should prevail. Tehuty (Hermes) sent Heru-Ur (Heracles) to Heru's aid, and he seized Set and knocked him flat on his face in front of the 42 natural laws, in the Hall of Justice in Eunu (Heliopolis). Set represented himself, while Tehuty was the advocate for Heru, who refused to speak. Finally, Set was found guilty of all charges and Tehuty placed Oser's throne over his back, declaring that Set had no authority over any living human from that day on, unless he gave him that right. Tehuty also declared Heru as King, giving to Set dominion over the oceans, deserts, and seas.

The story of Oser relates to the story of good, confirming that good overcomes evil, in this life and beyond. In the text in Plate 2, Oser is indicated as the son of Seb (earth) and Nut (heaven), since he was created by original cause, as a result of water from heaven mixing with soil. Egypt is described as the Red Land, in reference to the silt which comes when the Nile floods. The first Nile flood occurred when Set and his conspirators threw the chest carrying Oser's body into the Nile, and the violent splash caused the flooding, which has happened thereafter every year at the same time. Egypt is also described as the two lands, in reference to the north and south of Egypt, where the north is symbolized by the papyrus and the cobra, and the south by the lotus flower and the vulture.

Tehuty witnessed the birth and resurrection of Oser, and is described as bringing both *"the sweet winds to your nostrils"* and *"the beautiful wind to your face, which comes forth from Tumu"* (eternity). Oser's authority was established by Ptah, who ruled Egypt before the time of Oser for more than 9,000 years. This was inscribed on an iron slab on the great throne of Egypt, before Oser's birth.

PLATE 2

Tehuty had established within the boundaries of the natural laws the providence of nourishment and energy through water and earth. The laws of heaven and earth indicate the natural laws of existence, who were instructed by Tehuty to serve Heru, the son of Oser.

Hunefer also speaks of Oser's deeds, saying that all of the souls living in Egypt owe him the good which comes to them, until the end of time and that Oser's deeds will live on through future generations in the land of Egypt, forever. He mentions that Est cannot be separated from Oser since, in heaven, Est is embodied in the constellation of Sirius, or the Dog Star, while Oser is embodied in the constellation of Orion, and these two constellations reside beside each other. He adds that Oser's enemies, the people who embrace evil, cannot overthrow him because evil is always overcome by good, in this life and beyond.

The immortals, or the masters of the world as they were also called, gave praise to Oser: to them he had become the symbol of the cosmic man and the embodiment of all the good that exists within this life on earth. Oser's levels of awareness and consciousness increased because he followed the truth and obeyed the laws of nature, and his beauty arises from that which nourishes the soul. This, in turn, broadens the step; in other words, it causes the individual to acquire innate knowledge. Furthermore, Oser's authority came from a divine origin, since his father was earth and his mother was heaven, but he was able to unite both sides of himself (that which is above with that which is below). This total unity endowed him with complete authority. This is indicated in the form of the crook and flail, which he carried in his hands, and this was ordained even before Oser's birth, since he was crowned as a soul before he came forth on earth. The laws of nature honored him and traced their steps backward out of respect for him.

A tree-lined path near Meidum, Egypt. The Nile, giver of life, provides Egypt with plenty of lush vegetation.

PLATE 3

Translation

1 *"The laws see the strength of light and the victory of your majesty, and acknowledge it in their hearts.* **2** *Life is with you; providence is behind you. The truth was brought before you, so grant that I may be in fellowship with your majesty, as I was upon earth.* **3** *Let my soul be called out and let it be found on the side of the masters of the truth.* **4** *I have come into your divine city (the Dwat), during the epoch of time for all that belongs to the soul; the Ka and the Khu is within this region.* **5** *Divinity is the master of the truth, the master of providence, and the greatness of preparedness, and leads the whole of earth.* **6** *The South comes to you, sailing down the stream; the North, with rudders, in order to keep your daily festival, according to the divine command, which is the master of peace within it.* **7** *Does he not say, 'I care for the happiness of those who apply the divine truth in their life'?* **8** *He gives old age, ahead of its time, to those who commit sins, giving honor and a happy ending on earth, in Egypt, to those who apply the truth.* **9** *I have come to you, having done right and applied the truth. My spiritual heart (Saah) has not committed falsehood in life.* **10** *I offer you nothing but the truth.* **11** *I know what you live upon (the truth).* **12** *I have not done evil in this land (Egypt).* **13** *I have not defrauded anyone of his property.* **14** *I am one with Tehuty, the excellent scribe. My arms are pure. I am the destroyer of evil and scribe of the truth, and sins are an abomination to me.* **15** *Behold! You, with your writing pen (Tehuty), O master of limits (Oser), lord of laws,*

PLATE 3

Oser (Osiris) as the king of the afterlife, holding the crook, symbol of authority, and the flail, symbol of power, in his hands. He stands on the platform of truth.

giving the word of power, while passing through the two lands (Egypt). **16** *I am one with Tehuty, master of the truth, victorious, causing the weak to be victorious and avenging the wretched and oppressed against their oppressors.* **17** *I have vanquished darkness. I have performed mighty deeds. I have driven winds of life for Oser, in order to breathe in truth the north wind, as he comes forth from his mother's womb.* **18** *I granted that he might enter the abode of hidden life for the heart of the still heart, Oser, son of Nut, and his son, Heru, became victorious."*

Commentary

In Plate 3, Hunefer addresses Oser (Osiris), the King of the Dwat (netherworld), with a plea for himself, in which he indicates the righteousness of his deeds in life. He points out that he had followed the right way of living and had acquired awakening and purification in his life, according to the Egyptian spiritual doctrine of eternal life.

The goal of all living things is to vanquish the evil part of themselves, so that they can evolve to reach immortality. In the life of mankind, the struggle is between our two selves: the true self, which is called Dezmaa, and the false self, which is called Dezgreg. The personality is a false self, while the true personality is a true self, which is spiritual in nature. The struggle between these two selves creates doubts, fear, ignorance, anger, etc., and while these emotional qualities are not evil in themselves, they can lead to evil behavior. This need not happen. The sacred psychology of the Egyptians indicates that we all have an inner biological nature, which is persistent in its qualities but can change. Each person's Ka, or inner nature, is unique to the individual but also universal to all mankind. One can discover the universal qualities of one's own Ka and the specific qualities pertinent to each individual. This Ka is not innately evil, even if it has inherited some evil qualities from past lives, and it always comes to this life in a neutral state because the soul passes through the river of forgetfulness, prior to birth, and is born innocent.

It is important to enhance the qualities of the Ka, in order to guide one's life. If someone prevents the good qualities of their Ka from being expressed, or suppresses them, they will become sick, whether in a subtle or obvious way, sooner or later. The Ka is not strong but subtle and delicate, and can easily be overcome by habits, cultural pressure, and the behavioral attitude of the person in his or her daily life. The Ka does not give up easily, even in a sick person, but persists in subtle ways, in order to acquire actualization. Discipline and experience in life are necessary for people to gain insight into their own Ka. Sometimes bad experiences, such as frustration, pain, and tragedy, act as a teacher to awaken this Ka, in order for people to gain control over their inner impulses and the outside behavior that dictates our destiny.

It is important to learn more about people's natural tendencies, so that one can show them how to be good, how to be creative, how to respect themselves, and how to acquire self-realization. This was the essence of education in ancient Egypt. All children were tested at the age of five in the temples, in order to direct their destiny according to their own natural inclinations. According to one's Ka, each individual can be identified with one of seven classes of souls. The lowest class is that of the evil humans, such as mass-murderers, rapists, and so on, who live by the law of force. The second class is the little humans, who live by social laws, cheating, lying, gossiping, and hurting others, for no reason at all. The third class is that of the gentle humans, who live by the law of righteousness, since they are always striving to live the right way. This class of people is responsible for the advancement of any nation. The fourth class, masters, live by the law of love. The fifth, sages, live by the law of virtue. The sixth, the immortals, are governed by God directly and the law of death does not apply to them. The seventh class, the inhabitants of the kingdom of heaven, are also governed by God directly and live in the Milky Way, singing a song daily to the Creator.

Every evil act that we commit in this life causes us to despise ourselves. Everything that we do is recorded in our brain and ultimately will be copied onto our own soul at the time of its departure from the body. We have, therefore, to watch our feelings because they will change to be thoughts, our thoughts will become actions, our actions will become habits, and our habits will become our destiny.

Sacred psychology requires that we are true to our inner nature, and that we do not deny our true nature through weakness, for material gain or any other reason. When people hide their talents, like a painter who sells shoes instead, or an intelligent man who lives a life of stupidity, they perceive in a deep way that they have done wrong to themselves and despise themselves for it. From this self-punishment, neuroses may be born. However, if the individual's spirit is awakened, he or she could access a renewed courage, righteousness, and self-respect, and could, therefore, behave correctly. So, suffering and pain can awaken an individual to ask more questions, and these questions will be answered.

According to the doctrine of longevity or eternal life, everyone has to erect six pillars of healing in their own life. These six pillars are divided into two categories, which are known as the triangles of earth and heaven. When people have constructed the triangle of earth within themselves by applying the three pillars in this triangle, the force of heaven will descend upon them and the earthly and heavenly triangles will come together. In this way, it is possible for a human to achieve immortality. Healing acquired through the six pillars of healing is, in reality, a religious salvation, since the word "salvation" is derived from the Latin word *salvo*, which means "to heal." The human soul is born within the limits of a body and this condition is an imprisonment, for which the individual has to seek healing. The six pillars of healing facilitate this process of salvation for every human.

PLATE 3

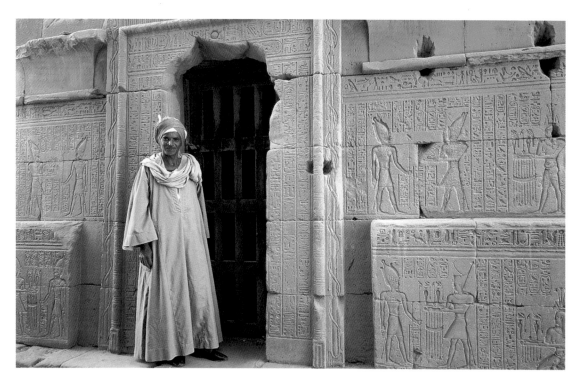

An attendant stands before the vault door of the temple of Emen at Karnak.

In the triangle of earth, the person must first achieve awakening, which can be achieved by the presence of a teacher or a master, where the individual can ask questions and they will be answered. It can also be acquired by persistence and discipline in applying what the master has instructed, and by vanquishing the possessive nature of the individual's psyche, using offering and sacrifice. A farmer, for example, should give the first crop of his land and an employee should offer his or her first month's salary for God's sake. By vanquishing their acquisitive nature, human beings are able to suspend the physical illusion, and this enables them ultimately to see their true nature and their real lives. Awakening can also be acquired by traumas and disasters, which act as teachers. For example, people may abuse their body until they have a heart attack, but it is this heart condition that will force them afterward to eat correctly, exercise, and offer prayers of thanks. In this instance, the sickness becomes a blessing, and so we should seek to gain at least one lesson from any problem. Another means of achieving awakening is through the state of bliss, or the moments in time where emotional conditions force one to suspend the material illusion and see reality.

When awakening has been achieved, we must purify our body and psyche. The cleansing process in ancient Egypt was achieved through the use of colonic irrigation, laxatives, and herbal combinations, designed to cleanse the digestive tract, blood, and internal organs of any impurities. The Egyptian people used to devote three days of each month for such cleansing, demonstrating that it is the most important step in the healing process. Without cleansing, the body, the soul, and spirits are trapped in darkness, like diamonds in mud. When you have cleansed your body of all the toxins and residues that have been accumulated, then you are ready to cleanse your thoughts and feelings, through what are called the "black and white mirrors."

The black mirror is the process of contemplating your negative qualities and all the bad events that you have experienced in your life. This period of contemplation takes from three to seven days. Having recalled all the pain and suffering, you then release it and forgive yourself and everyone else who ever did you wrong. The white mirror is the process of contemplating all the positive qualities that you have and all the good things that you have experienced in this life. When you have recalled all of these pleasures and joys, you should release this energy and say with intent, "I exchange the pleasures of earth for the pleasures

PLATE 3

of heaven." In completing these two processes of the black and white mirrors, you will have released and freed your entire internal energy resources. This process is of paramount importance in the purification of one's own psyche (soul and mind).

After the purification has been completed, the process of activation must be applied, which marks the beginning of the healing process and the acquisition of good health. It is achieved by the application of the Egyptian physical culture, which includes breathing exercises, stretching exercises, power exercises, postures, and warrior training (Sebek-Kha). The breathing exercises activate the blood circulation, the postures activate the nervous systems, and the power and stretching exercises activate the muscular and skeletal systems, while the warrior training brings about unity between the four elementary systems (cardiovascular, nervous, muscular, and skeletal).

These three pillars (awakening, purification, and activation) form the earthly triangle. When this has been activated, the heavenly triangle comes into operation. This includes the process of rejuvenation. When the body is working correctly, the internal and external energy can be fully utilized. The body then starts to create new skin and tissues in all its organs and muscles, which takes about 15 years. Then follows the process of life renewal, where the body experiences a state of heat and light, leading to the renewal of teeth, nails, and bones. This process takes about ten years. Finally, the state of longevity is achieved, which assures permanent health and increases the lifespan of an individual until they reach the state of immortality. There is no time limit for this stage; it depends upon the individual concerned and some people never reach it.

The text in Plate 3 talks about providence being behind the individual, which means mundane life, then indicates that life is with the person, meaning eternal life. It also mentions that the South comes to Oser, sailing down the stream, implying the flow of the Nile's water northward, while the North uses rudders because it travels against the stream. This implies that the entire population of Egypt participates in the praise and memory of Oser's deeds.

A picture of the enclosure of the temple of Karnak, taken from above the sacred lake. Karnak was the beginner's school of initiation.

PLATE 4

Illustration 1

The scene of the judgment of the heart of the deceased. The judgment scene in this papyrus acts as an introduction to the chapters of *The Book of the Dead*, which follow thereafter. The illustrations which are depicted above the judgment scene show Hunefer kneeling before the natural laws in an adoration pose. Below, Hunefer is led by Enpu (Anubis), son of Nebt-Het, to the scales of justice, where his heart, the symbol of his deeds, is weighed against the feather of truth, the symbol for the spiritual laws. In the upper register, 14 laws are depicted and Hunefer kneels before them in an adoration posture. These are 14 of the 42 judges of the dead, who are also a representation of the 42 natural laws in nature. Each of the laws is identified by a name, written in front of the image. These laws are: Ra, Tum, Shu, Tefnut, Seb, Nut, Heru-Ur, Est, Nebt-Het, Hu, Sa, Uat-Resut, Uat-Meht, and Uat-Ementet.

Above the beam that supports the scales, a figure of Maat is depicted, emblem of the truth and law, as a female-headed figure, with a feather over her head. Enpu kneels upon a pylon, testing the indicator or

PLATE 4

tongue of the balance. The monster, Ammit, the devourer of the dead, stands close to the pillar of the scales, in front of Enpu. He has the head of a crocodile, implying light and knowledge, the hind part of a hippopotamus, indicating rebirth, and the middle part of a lion, indicating vigilance, strength, and awakening. Tehuty (Hermes) stands on the right side of the monster Ammit, holding a scribe's palette and a reed pen, recording the result of the judgment.

Illustration 2

Hunefer has been judged and found just. He is led into the presence of Oser, the embodiment of good, by Oser's son, Heru, who is depicted with a falcon head, implying his solar nature.

Translation

Speech of Tehuty

Tehuty, the lord of divine words, said: "I am making just the name of the royal scribe, Hunefer, who is united with Oser. His heart came forth on the scales of justice and evil was not found."

Speech of Heru

Heru, the avenger and excellent heir of his father, said: "Behold! I am bringing to you Hunefer, who is united with Oser. He has been judged by the scales of justice and the indicator of the balance rests upon its place, where it should be."

Hunefer, addressing his heart

1 Chapter of the royal scribe, Hunefer, addressing his heart, victoriously: "My heart, heart of my mother (repeat this twice), heart of my existence, may no resistance occur against me in my judgment. 2 May no repulsion arise against me on the part of the divine judges. 3 May you not be separated from me in the presence of the one who operates the scales of justice. 4 You are my Ka within my body, which forms and strengthens my limbs. 5 May you come forth to the place of happiness, where I shall dwell for years to come. 6 May no disgrace come upon my name on the day of judgment. 7 May the nourishment of life be granted to me in the house of life-giving, and may my heart be gladdened in the house of harmony."

The avenue of ram-headed sphinxes, before the temple of Karnak, which represent the sacrifice of the human souls.

Commentary

Plate 4 contains an illustration and description of the day of judgment after death.

Before someone dies, a process of psychic photography takes place, whereby all of one's life experiences and collective memory form an imprint on one's soul from the cerebrum memory. Then the soul departs, leaving the body lifeless. It leaves in the form of a spiral of energy, commonly called a halo, and so the eyes of the deceased are always found looking upward, in a frozen condition. The individual is very aware of this process and his tongue freezes because of the overwhelming effect on him. It is said that people are asleep and when they die they wake up.

On the night of the individual's death, their resurrection or judgment takes place. The deceased stands in front of the 42 natural laws or judges and the king of the afterworld, Oser (Osiris), giving a complete account of their life. No lies can be told then, because you see your whole life played out in front of you, with all that you have said and done. Because of this, in this Plate Hunefer addresses his own heart, asking that it would not stand against him on the day of judgment. Afterward, the deceased person judges himself, deciding upon his next form of reincarnation and the type of life that he will lead after death. The deceased, therefore, becomes his own judge, witness, and prosecution.

Souls who did not do well become subject to the cycle of Oser in the Orion constellation and inhabit an appointed place in heaven, awaiting their time to return to their next embodiment. This process of reincarnation, however, is not indefinite, since each soul has only five lives in which to come back to earth. After that, it becomes one of the lost souls in the Dwat or the purgatory state. The souls who did do well go to the Fields of Peace, or Sekhet-Hetep, where they are taught by other enlightened souls and inhabit the level appropriate to the level of evolution that they achieved during their life. Some of these souls become one with the perfected souls and do not return to earth; others are the souls of masters and sages, who come back to life to fulfill a specific purpose, and so this process is known as conscious reincarnation. The souls of the masters spend an average of 2,500 years in the Fields of Peace before returning to earth; the souls of the sages an average of 10,000 years. They return to earth among one of the four original races of mankind, the Africans, Asians, Europeans, and Egyptians, in a cycle of 600 years for each race.

In Plate 4, the two principles who pronounce Hunefer's final judgment are Tehuty, the principle of knowledge, purity, reflection, and divine reason, and Heru, the principle of power, strength, conviction, and obedience.

A mural from the tomb of Ramses II, representing a portion of the life in the Dwat (netherworld).

The third pyramid of Giza, which was used
to enhance the physical power of the initiate.

PLATE 5

Illustrations

Oser, the head of the West (the place of departed souls), is seated on a throne within a shrine. The shrine is surmounted by 28 cobras, with sun disks over their heads, representing the life of Oser, who lived and ruled for 28 years, dying at the age of 28. Oser holds the crook, Heqa, in his right hand and the flail, Nekhekh, in his left, symbols of the North and South and the sovereignty and dominion over them. He is swathed in white linen, indicating that his authority is not in the mundane world (Ta) but over the dominion of departed souls in the Dwat (netherworld). Behind him stand his two sisters, Est (Isis) and Nebt-Het (Nephthys), and a line of text is written in front of them: *"We are your sisters, Est and Nebt-Het."*

Oser's throne stands over a sacred and divine pool of water, from which a lotus flower springs. Above the flower and in front of Oser are the four sons of Heru, who act as the guardians of the cardinal points of the human temple (body). These four sons of Heru represent the lungs (to the north), the intestine (to the south), the liver (to the west), and the stomach (to the east). Their names, which are written above their heads, are: Hapi (lungs), Qeb-Sen-F (intestine), Meste (liver), Dwa-Mut-F (stomach). In front

An avenue of sphinxes at Memphis.

of Oser is written: *"Oser, the head of Ementet, divine and great principle."*

In the top left-hand corner of the shrine is the right eye of Heru, with the wings of the vulture and claws of a falcon, indicating the victory and evolution of human consciousness. One of the falcon's claws holds a Shen, the sign of infinity, which means "that which is encircled by the Sun will always be eternal." The other claw holds the sword of truth, which is made out of a feather.

Commentary

Plate 5 does not contain any text, except that which is shown in the illustration.

The illustration in Plate 5 represents Oser as a symbol for every living human, in total control of his life and guarded by two invisible guardians, one to the right, represented by Est, and one to the left, represented by Nebt-Het.

PLATE 6

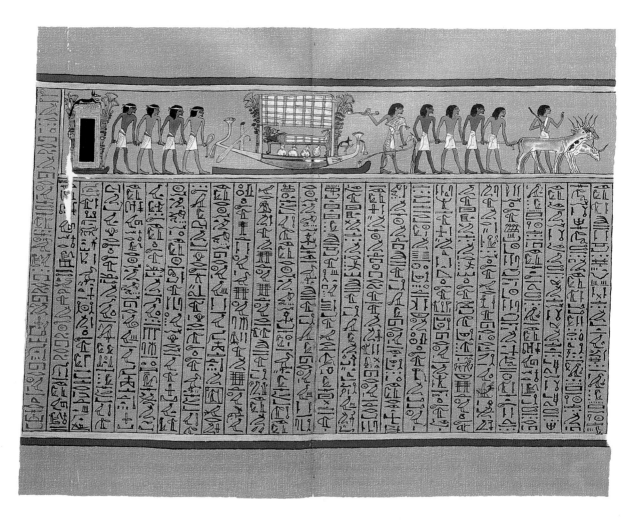

Illustrations

Plates 6 and 7 portray Hunefer's funeral procession to the tomb. In the center of Plate 6, his mummy is shown lying in a funeral coffin and mounted on a boat, whose runners are drawn by three bulls. On the left-hand side, in the upper register, four people are pulling along a dark doorway, over which Enpu (Anubis), the son of Nebt-Het, is prostrated on a sledge: In front of the mummy stands the High Priest, holding incense in his right hand and pouring water from a jar held in his left hand. In front of him, four people are pulling the rope that connects the coffin to the oxen, while another man leads the procession, walking alongside the oxen. The emblem of the jackal-headed Enpu, who stands between the visible and the invisible, is depicted in the bows of the boat over a standard.

PLATE 6

Translation

1 *The beginning of the chapters of* The Book of Coming Forth by Day *and of praises and glorification of entrance into and exit out of the netherworld, shining in the beautiful West.* **2** *This is to be said on the day of burial, upon going into the netherworld, after coming forth to life.* **3** *The scribe, Hunefer, beloved of Oser, said:* "Homage to you, the head of Ementet! **4** *Behold, Tehuty, the King of eternity! He is with me.* **5** *I am the great lord of the boat of life. I have fought for you.* **6** *I have become one with those laws of nature, the divine masters, who cause Oser to be victorious on the day of weighing words and deeds.* **7** *Oser, I am your advocate. I am one of those natural laws.* **8** *I was born from heaven and worked with the natural laws to shut away the enemies of Oser.* **9** *Heru, I am your advocate!* **10** *I fought for you and defeated your enemies, in your honor.* **11** *I am Tehuty, who makes Oser victorious over his enemies on the day of weighing words and deeds in the dwelling place of the great ones in Eunu.* **12** *I am stability and the son of stability.* **13** *I was conceived in the town of stability (Djedu) and I was born in the same town.* **14** *I witnessed the mourners and wailers for Oser in Egypt, and Oser was made victorious over his enemies.* **15** *Ra and Tehuty ordained for Oser to be victorious over his enemies.* **16** *I was with Heru on the day when Oser, the still of heart, was clothed and washed, unbolting the door of hidden things in the land of Rastau.* **17** *I was with Heru, protecting the shoulder of Oser, which was left by Set in the city of Sekhem.* **18** *I went forth and came in peace out of the flames, on the day when the enemies of Oser were destroyed in Sekhem.* **19** *I was with Heru on the days of the festivals of Oser, making the offerings on the sixth day of the festival of Dnet in*

The impressive pyramids of Giza in Cairo still hold a great fascination today.

the city of Eunu. **20** *I am the purity priest in the city of stability and I am the lion in the temple of Oser, elevating the earthly existence to heaven.* **21** *I can see in truth the hidden things in the spiritual path of Rastau.* **22** *I am able to read the ritual book of the soul in the city of stability.* **23** *I am the ritual priest in his glory.* **24** *I am the great chief of the service on the day of celebrating the coming of light and life by placing the Hennu boat of Sokar on the sledge.* **25** *I have received the honor of digging the divine foundation of the temple in the city of Suten-Khenen.* **26** *O you, who cause perfected souls to enter the house of Oser, may you cause the perfected soul of the scribe, Hunefer, to enter the house of Oser, victorious, with you."*

PLATE 6

Commentary

Plate 6 forms the introduction to *The Book of the Dead*. Hunefer addresses Oser (Osiris), indicating his association and unity with the natural laws and recording his deeds in resisting evil and conquering the enemies of good. He points out that his soul witnessed the past events of the struggle between good and evil and that he is entering the realm of the Dwat (netherworld) with knowledge of the foundation and construction of the spiritual realm, since he was the priest responsible for the rituals relating to the spiritual realm. He mentions the path of Sokar, implying that, during his lifetime, he erected the six pillars of healing, which lead to this spiritual path of eternal life. He also mentions the destruction of the enemies of Oser in the city of Sekhem. This indicates that the struggle between good and evil occurs in the human energy, which is called Sekhem or the electromagnetic current. This struggle, therefore, takes place energetically within the individual's psyche and so the vanquishing of evil itself can only be achieved on that level.

Hunefer mentions the land of Rastau, which is the entrance to the realm of the Dwat. He addresses Oser, saying that he was with his son, Heru, on the days when he attended the festivals of his father in the city of Eunu (Heliopolis), during the festival of Dnet. This implies that he knows his past reincarnations and that his lineage, even in remote times, was always associated with the principle of good. He mentions that he was conceived, born, and became the purity priest in the city of Djedu. The word *Djed*, or sometimes *Djedu*, implies stability and a good foundation for the truth.

The introduction concludes with a heartfelt plea from Hunefer to be able to enter the house of Oser (Dwat) victorious, with Oser's help.

The sunset was very important to the ancient Egyptians. They saw it as a symbol of death and resurrection.

PLATE 7

Illustrations

The funerary procession of Hunefer continues until it reaches the tomb. In the illustration on the left, the procession is led by the Kher-Heb, or the recital priest, who narrates the funeral service. He is followed by two mourners, six wailing women (one of whom is bending forward), and a servant, who carries Hunefer's staff, chair, and box of personal belongings. On the right, a

PLATE 7

group of men is performing the last rites. In front of the door of the tomb stands the mummy of Hunefer, with Enpu (Anubis), son of Nebt-Het, embracing it from behind. At the feet of the mummy, Hunefer's wife and daughter are bidding farewell to the body.

Behind them stand two priests. One of them is holding four jars of ointment up to the face of the mummy; the other priest is holding in his right hand a Nu, the instrument of opening the mouth, which has the same shape as the seven stars of Ursa-Major in heaven, known as the constellation of the thigh of Set, or Mes-Khent. This instrument was made out of iron, the metal of Set, which is cold and compassionless. In his left hand, the second priest is holding another instrument and he is about to touch the mouth and eyes of the mummy with it. Behind the priest there is an offering table, and standing behind this is the High Priest, dressed in a leopard skin. He holds a water jar in his right hand and a censer (a vessel in which incense is burned) in his left hand.

In the lower register of the illustration, a cow and her calf are portrayed on a platform, representing life renewal. Two men stand in front of them, bearing in their hands offerings of a jar of ointment and the thigh of a bull. A box of personal belongings lies in front of them, with an offering table and another table upon it. There are water jars, jars of ointment, the instrument Nu and other ceremonial instruments, boxes of purification, and a bundle of spices. On the round stele (standing block), which stands close to the tomb, the deceased is seen standing in adoration before Oser (Osiris). Below him are 11 lines of text:

"May Oser, the governor of Ementet, the lord of eternity, who exists in the everlasting things, lord of praises and the leader of the company of the nine laws, send Enpu, the dweller in the city of embalmment and governor of the divine house, so that he may grant Hunefer, who is united with Oser, the power to enter into and come forth from the underworld, to follow Oser in all his festivals of the new year, to receive offerings of bread (life), and to come forth into the presence of divinity."

Translation

1 *May Oser grant peace to you, the governor of the West, lord of eternity, possessor of everlasting things, lord of praises and head of the company of the nine laws (Paut).* **2** *Hail, Enpu, who dwells in the town of embalmment as a great principle, governor of the divine house.* **3** *May they grant an entrance and exit in the netherworld to the followers of Oser, who made all of his festivals at the new year and gave offerings, in order to come forth in the presence of the divine spirit of Oser, as Hunefer has done.* **4** *The chapter of opening the mouth of the statue of the royal scribe, Hunefer, while he is facing south, with all the events of his past lives compiled behind him, like a mountain of sand.* **5** *The ceremonial priest Kher-Heb says to the High Priest (Sem), while going backward behind him four times and carrying four jars of water: "You are pure; Heru is pure, as you are. You are pure; Tehuty is pure, as you are. You are pure, Sep is pure, as you are. You are pure; Seb is pure, as you are. Pure (repeat this twice); you are four times pure. Here comes Hunefer, who is united with Oser, victoriously. You possess an essence of the essence of Heru. You possess an essence of the essence of Tehuty. You possess an essence of the essence of Sep. You possess an essence of the essence of Seb."*

Commentary

Plate 7 explains the procedures and the words that should be uttered during the ritual of opening the mouth of the deceased. The High Priest entreats Oser, as head of the Paut, to grant Hunefer peace. He also entreats the laws and principles of the Dwat to grant an entrance and exit in the netherworld to the followers of Oser, or good, who have recorded their faith and conviction in their book of deeds. Both the High Priest and the ritual priest emphasize Hunefer's purity, repeating four times each that Hunefer is pure, and they compare his purity to that of Heru, son of Oser, Tehuty (Hermes), Seb (earth), and Sep, who is the divine falcon, the symbol of the soul and all that belongs to the realm of the soul. They also mention that Hunefer possesses the essence of Heru, Tehuty, Seb, and Sep. This implies that Hunefer has lived by the natural laws of existence and become one with them, acquiring total unity.

The mouth of the deceased is closed when he dies and opened again for him after death. The deceased pleads that his mouth would be open, meaning that his memory would be restored to him after the silence of death. The ritual of opening the mouth was one of the most profound secrets of ancient Egypt, performed at the entry to the tomb as well as in the Dwat by Ptah, the first craftsman on earth. The divine intelligence, which has been cultivated in life, becomes active after death and is in favor of the deceased.

This Plate emphasizes the Doctrine of Purification, an integral part of the Egyptian spiritual doctrines, which here implies purification of the body, soul, spirit, and mind. Once the divine intelligence is restored, the deceased collects all the utterances of protection, or words of power, which help him to overcome his oppositions in the Dwat.

PLATE 7

Elaborately carved columns in the hypostyle hall of the temple of Edfu, dedicated to Heru-Ur (Horus).

PLATE 8

Illustrations

Plates 8, 9, 10, and 11 constitute Chapter 17 of *The Book of the Dead*. The illustration, therefore, extends across the length of the four plates in the upper register. Plate 8, on the left-hand side, begins with the symbol of the West, Ementet. This is composed of a loaf of bread (symbol of life-giving) and, on top of it, the feather of truth (symbol of law and universal order) and the falcon (symbol of the dominion and realm of spiritual laws).

Under the loaf of bread is the symbol of action, which is depicted by the linen fold. This implies that the West (Ementet) is concerned with action, relevant to life, and governed by the truth.

Below this, there is a mountain, the symbol of communion. On one side of the mountain is a water jar (symbol of harmony in life) and on the other side, a loaf of bread (symbol of life-giving and everlasting providence). Hunefer stands before the symbol of the

PLATE 8

West, looking backward at his past life. Above his head is written: *"Beloved of Oser, Hunefer, victorious."*

Hunefer is also standing after the symbol of the West, looking forward toward his future life and holding a staff in his left hand, which is the symbol of knowledge of good and evil. Then he is seen seated in a shrine, with a chequerboard in front of him, which represents all the events of his life and its consequences. He is looking at all of his deeds. In front of him, again, is written: *"Beloved of Oser, Hunefer, victorious."*

Then Hunefer's soul emerges in an adoration pose, in the form of a stork with a human head, expressing the transmigration of the soul. In front of this "Ba" bird, the soul of Hunefer, is written: *"The soul of the beloved of Oser, Hunefer."*

The scene in the middle depicts Hunefer kneeling before Aker, the symbol of time. This symbol expresses the past, in the form of a lion facing west, the future, in the form of a lion facing east, and the present moment, in the form of the rising sun above a mountain. On the other side of Aker, Oser (Osiris) awaits the arrival of Hunefer. The last scene in Plate 8 depicts Hunefer kneeling in an adoration pose before an offering table, where the Benu bird (phoenix) is standing, the symbol of the regeneration of the soul.

Translation

1 *Here begin the praises and glorification of coming forth and going into the beautiful West (Dwat).* **2** *On the day of transformation into all that pleases the deceased, after reckoning his life's deeds in the Hall of Justice.* **3** *In coming forth as a living soul, behold, Hunefer, who is united with Oser, traveling in his boat, with the deeds that he accomplished upon earth.* **4** *The words of the Creator will come to pass.* **5** *Hunefer, who is united with Oser, said: "I am united with the Creator through His creations. I am associated with the almighty One in the water of Nu.* **6** *I am the light, which rose in the beginning of time and created His own authority."* **7** *What does this mean? It is the light that rose, generating youth and royalty.* **8** *The four cardinal points did not exist, nor did those who dwell in the City of Eight.* **9** *I am the great principle, who created Himself.* **10** *It is the water of Nu, which was created by the power of sound; the water from which the nine laws came into existence.* **11** *What does this mean? It is the principle of light, who created, from His members, all the laws of nature.* **12** *I am the one who has no equal among the laws.* **13** *What does this mean? It is Tumu, who comes forth through the sun disk; in other words, it is the light, which rises in the eastern horizon of heaven.* **14** *I know yesterday and tomorrow.* **15** *What does this mean? Oser is yesterday and light is tomorrow.* **16** *It is the day on which the enemies of the master of limits were destroyed by his divine son, Heru.* **17** *In other words, it is the day when the festivals of Oser were established.* **18** *The battle took place among the natural laws.* **19** *Oser was ordained by decree to be the master and lord of the West.* **20** *What does this mean? It is the West, where the souls of the natural laws were created, and Oser was ordained to be the lord of the West.* **21** *In other words, the West is the place of light, where every law must rise.* **22** *Every law must do battle with the illusion, which exists therein, and I know the great principle, who resides therein.* **23** *What does this mean? It is Oser; in other words, his name is light.* **24** *He is the begetter of light.* **25** *I am the Benu bird (phoenix) in Eunu.* **26** *I am the keeper of the book of*

things that are and things that will be. **27** What does this mean? *It is Oser; in other words, it is the dead body of Oser, namely the tomb of his enemies.* **28** *It is the dead body of Oser, which is the place of eternal and everlasting things.* **29** *The day is everlasting and the night is eternity, which exists in the head of every man.* **30** What does this mean? *It is the divine Heru, the avenger of his father.* **31** *The truth manifests itself through reincarnations.* **32** *Est and Nebt-Het cause these reincarnations to take place.* **33** *They exist in all limits, as the protectresses of incarnations.* **34** *In other words, Est and Nebt-Het are the two great laws within the divine transformation of the father of all, Tumu.* **35** *Est and Nebt-Het are the two hidden eyes of God, in the realm of the soul. It is the royal scribe, Hunefer, who exists in this land, victoriously.* **36** *He has come to his everlasting city.* **37** What does this mean? *It is the divine horizon of the Father of all, Tumu.* **38** *I have made an end to my mistakes and vanquished my sins.* **39** What does this mean? *It is the severing of the corruptible part of Hunefer, who is united with Oser, victoriously, and the smiting away of all evil things that cling onto him.* **40** What does this mean? *It is the purification on the day of his birth.*

The remains of the grandiose entrance to the temple of Karnak.

The temple of Abu Simbel, which was built by Ramses II.

Commentary

Plate 8 describes what happened to the soul of the deceased in the realm of the Dwat (netherworld), after he had been judged in the Hall of Justice. The deceased comes forth in a purified and glorious form, having shed all the evil residues that clung to him in his earthly existence. Now, he does not just associate with the laws and principles of eternal life but assumes their shape and state of being, and so he utters, "I am associated with the almighty One in the water of Nu," which takes the deceased back to the beginning of time. He even associates with God, saying that he is God Himself; in other words, that he has become one with the Creator. He declares, therefore, that he is the original light of God, "which rose in the beginning of time and created His own authority," adding that none existed at that time, except the light of God, who created Himself. Then, the water of Nu was created by the power of sound, from which the nine laws of natural existence (Paut) came forth. He mentions that God manifests Himself in our earthly existence through the sunlight, which gives life to everything. He also relates that the Dwat, or the West, is the place of light and the realm of the soul. Oser is the King of that realm and all souls have to do battle with the illusion of living within it.

The deceased has passed through to the realm of light in the constellation of Orion, which is the house of Oser. In his new, purified condition, he identifies himself as the "keeper of the book of things that are and things that will be." He declares that God, who is the truth, manifests Himself through reincarnation; in other words, He manifests Himself through His creations. He also mentions that it is Est (Isis) and Nebt-Het (Nephthys), residing in the constellation of Sirius (Sepdu), who cause reincarnation to take place, adding that they "exist in all limits as the protectresses of incarnations." It is for this reason that we find Est and Nebt-Het standing behind Oser in the illustrations of Plate 5 (see page 72). He describes them as the two hidden eyes of God, in the realm of the soul.

The Plate concludes with the deceased acknowledging that he has made an end to his mistakes and vanquished his sins by severing the corruptible part of himself and becoming able to unite with Oser, the symbol of good, victoriously. He mentions the Doctrine of Purification, which starts from the conception of man and at his birth.

Plate 9

Illustrations

In Plate 9, the scene in the upper register continues from that of Plate 8. On the left-hand side, Heru, the son of Oser, is depicted with the red and white crown of Egypt on his head, and the crook and flail, symbols of authority over the North and South regions, emerging from his knees. The mummy of Hunefer is placed in a shrine, protected by a female falcon on each side, one of whom represents Est (Isis) and the other Nebt-Het (Nephthys). Hunefer is then seen kneeling in front of the two cobras of the North and South. Behind them is a table of offerings, and also the eye of Heru, with a divinity stretching its hands over it. Behind this is Heh, the symbol for millions of years, who stretches out his right arm over a pool of fire, while looking at another pool of water. These two pools are called Maat and

PLATE 9

Hesmen, and the symbols imply that Hunefer's soul is purified by fire and water.

On the right-hand side, Hunefer and Nasha, his wife, emerge greater in size, as if to say that they are emerging larger than life, victoriously. In her right hand, Nasha holds a sistrum (a musical instrument), the symbol of resisting evil in life, and in her left hand, a papyrus plant, the symbol of life and prosperity. Hunefer stands in an adoration pose. In front of Nasha is written: *"Mistress of the house, Nasha."* In front of Hunefer is written: *"Beloved of Oser, royal scribe of the king of the two lands (Maat-Men-Ra) Hunefer, victorious."*

Above the heads of Hunefer and Nasha, a few lines of text are written:

"Homage to you, masters of the West, O company of the nine laws in the netherworld. May they give entrance and exit to me. May I not be turned back at the doors of the masters of the Dwat. May I receive life nourishment on the altar table of the masters of eternity for the Ka of the royal scribe, Hunefer, who is united with Oser, victoriously. May life nourishment be given to me in the house of nourishment and life harmony in the house of harmony. Behold! The overseer of the royal cattle, Hunefer, who is united with Oser, victoriously."

An example of the typical fertile farmland to be found in Egypt today. Although the flood water of the Nile is no longer depended on for watering purposes, Egypt is still a flourishing agricultural center.

The deceased, sailing to the area of Abydos, the entrance to the Dwat.

Translation

1 *"I achieved purification of my body and soul in the time of my youth, when other people were busy with the dazzling illusion of life.* **2** *What does this mean? The essence of it is the one mighty ocean (God); other names for this mighty ocean are leadership and fellowship within the house of greatness.* **3** *In other words, it is the ocean of millions of years of knowledge; that is to say, it is the creator of millions of years of knowledge.* **4** *As for the great divine principle within this mighty ocean, it is light itself.* **5** *I have lived my life, knowing the spiritual and physical laws.* **6** *What does this mean? It is the northern path of immortality (Rastau). It is the gateway to the southern path, which binds together the spiritual bodies after passing away from the tomb. As for the spiritual and physical laws, they exist in Abdu.* **7** *Namely, it is the road that God, the father of all, ordained for the souls in the Fields of Peace, where celestial nourishment is produced as the sustenance for all the divine souls underlying the myriads of forms. It is the northern gate of the Dwat.* **8** *Namely, it is the open gate, which Tumu has ordained in the eastern horizon of heaven.* **9** *O begetters of life, grant me your help, so that I may become a divine principle among you.* **10** *What* does this mean? *It is humanity, which came forth from the creative aspect of God, after He had formed all living things from Himself.* **11** *They came into existence as the living laws, who follow the light of God, with knowledge, in the course of every day.* **12** *I have filled Hunefer, who is united with Oser, with triumph and the power generated from the eye of Heru, within the battle between good and evil.* **13** What does this mean? *It all started with the battle between Heru and Set, when evil blinded the face of Heru with all manner of bad things and Heru castrated Set, rendering him impotent, using the power of knowledge itself. I became aware of evil at that time, when storms took place in the sky.* **14** What does this mean? *It is the right eye of God in nature, which rages against evil.* **15** *Behold, Tehuty, who raises up awareness and brings it forth!"*

Commentary

Plate 9 reveals that Hunefer acquired purification in his body and soul during his youth, while other people were busy with futile things. The question is raised as to what this means; in other words, what is it that caused him to follow this path. Hunefer replies that faith in the almighty God, the Creator of the universe, inspired him in this quest. He also indicates that he spent his life trying to understand the spiritual and physical laws and that, in the course of attaining this knowledge, he discovered the future of the soul and what happens to it after death. He also discovered that the path of immortality, Rastau, is the gateway for the southern journey of the soul, in which the individual becomes a perfected soul, after shedding everything that belonged to earth.

He mentions that the journey of the soul begins in Sekhet-Hetep and Sekhet-Earu, or the Fields of Peace, known as the Elysian Fields in the Hellenic period of Egyptian history. In reality, there are two fields of peace: lower and upper. The soul of the deceased arrives at Mount Hetep, or the mount of glory, prior to its entry into the judgment hall, and this exists in the lower domain of Oser, or the Orion constellation. There are two stages of ascent from the lower field of peace to the upper, each marked by a ladder: the ladder of Sut, or Set (Satan), which is a representation of the ascent of the soul to the land of darkness, and the ladder of Heru, the ascent of the soul to the land of light. The deceased, therefore, says, *"I raise my ladder up to the sky that I may behold the laws."*

Hunefer entreats the begetters of life to grant him help, so that he may become one with them. During his lifetime, he was filled with knowledge, which stemmed from awareness of the battle between good (represented by Heru) and evil (represented by Set). He mentions that the struggle between good and evil always exists upon earth and adds that evil throws so many bad things in the face of the good, in order to render him blind, indicating the dazzling illusions of life. Good, however, has rendered evil impotent, which means that evil has no authority over any human, unless they gave him that authority.

At the end of Plate 9, Hunefer mentions that he became aware of evil when, at the beginning of time, storms took place in the sky. Upon seeing the power of good coming through the Sun, which acts as the right eye of God in nature, vanquishing all darkness and giving life to everything, he realized that good will always overcome evil and that Tehuty (Hermes) set the foundation of the knowledge of good in the hearts of mankind since the beginning of time.

PLATE 10

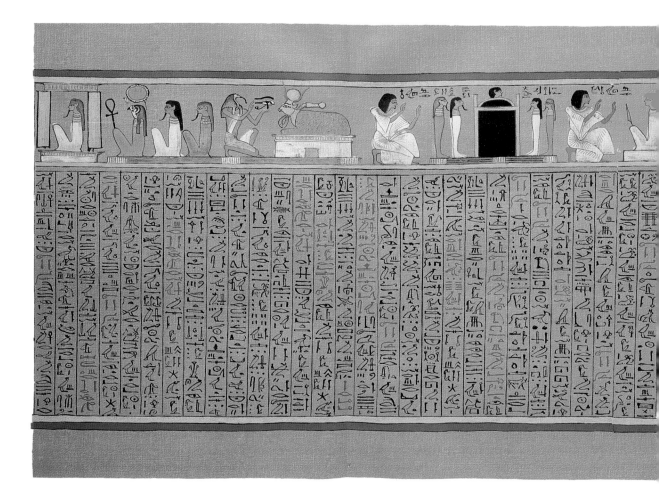

Illustrations

The illustration from Plate 9 continues in Plate 10. On the upper left-hand side there is a law within a shrine, followed by Ra, the light of God in nature, and the two laws of day and night, all of which are facing Hunefer's past life. Then, Tehuty (Hermes) is depicted in a kneeling posture, holding the right eye of Heru, son of Oser (Osiris), in his left hand and, in front of him, the divine cow, Meh-Urit, which is the symbol of eternal providence. Then, Hunefer is depicted in front of his own spiritual faculties, which are the four supporters of the cardinal points and the symbols of the four main organs in the human body (the liver, lungs, intestine, and stomach). The name of each is written above their heads. The principle of light emerges from a black sarcophagus in the center, indicating the emergence and rebirth of Hunefer's soul. Finally, Hunefer is portrayed kneeling before the gate to the unknown.

90

PLATE 10

Translation

1 *Hunefer is given life, prosperity, and health, without any sins.* Namely, *this is achieved by the power of the divine vision in its compassionate state of being, when the principle of knowledge (Tehuty) awakens and cleanses the inner being.* **2** *I have seen God's light in nature, born of yesterday from the eastern side of heaven, and the strength of this light is my strength.* **3** What does this mean? *It is the water of heaven;* namely, *it is the image of the rising Sun, the eye of God in nature, which is born every day.* **4** *O divine heaven, this eye is the eye of light, and therefore, the scribe, Hunefer, who is united with Oser, victoriously comes forth as one of these great principles, who are in the fellowship of Heru, ordained for him who loves his master.* **5** What does this mean? *These are the liver (Mesty), the lungs (Hapi), the stomach (Dua-Mut-F), and the intestine (Qeb-Sen-F). Homage to you, masters of justice and truth, divine beings, who are the supporters of good and cause all weaknesses to be annihilated in divine harmony.* **6** *Grant me that I may unite with you and destroy all weaknesses, which are mine, according to that which is ordained for the seven glorious spirits of nature.* **7** *Those spirits, who are among the followers of the lord of divine circumstances, have made the invisible realm their place of existence, particularly on the day of coming forth and stepping into the unknown.* **8** What does this mean? *They are the masters of justice and truth, Tehuty and Oser, the masters of the western path.* **9** *The divine spirits who support Oser are: the liver, the lungs, the stomach, and the intestine. These are the same spirits who support the constellation of the Big Bear in northern heaven. Those who cause the destruction of sins are in the*

An imposing avenue of sphinx-like rams in front of the great temple of Emen at Luxor.

fellowship of the law of harmony in the constellation of the Small Bear and they are part of the light of God in nature. **10** Namely, the power of the divine fire follows Oser to consume the souls of his enemies. **11** As for the sins of the scribe of the divine offering, Hunefer, who is united with Oser, has become victorious, even as he emerged from his mother's womb. **12** As for the divine seven spirits in nature—Mesty, Hapi, Dua-Mut-F, Qeb-Sen-F, Maa-Etf-F, Khenty-Beq-F, and Heru-Khenty-Maa—they were appointed by Enpu as the protectors of the innocent body of good. **13** There are also seven glorious, powerful laws, who are responsible for the protection and purification of Oser. These are: Nedh, Eakedenu-Kedenu, Nen-Redy-N-F-Bes, Khenty-Heh-F, Saq-Her-Emy-Unnut-F, Dsher-Maa-Emy, and Het-Ens. They are the fire, which comes forth in peace, with vision, brought in the night every day. **14** The chief of these divine beings is Heru, the avenger of his father. **15** As for the day of stepping into the invisible world, it is said by the principle of light that the condition of the soul can only be known when it comes to Ementet (the West) and discovers what has been decreed for it there. **16** What does this mean? It is Oser, who is in the city of stability, causing the souls of light to embrace one another and inviting other souls to reside amongst the spirits of light and justice. **17** As for these two spirits of light and justice (Thafy), they are created by Heru, the avenger of his father, and Heru, the causer of insight. Namely, they are his double soul within light and justice. They are the soul of light, the soul of good, the soul that exists in air and moisture. This double soul also exists in the human body. **18** I am like the cat, which is in constant struggle to achieve joy and happiness.

PLATE 10

The sun at noon, representing the
fire of life and the power of youth.

Commentary

Plate 10 explains the result of Hunefer's salvation in life and its outcome, which gave him *"life, prosperity, and health, without any sins."* This was achieved by the power of divine vision or intelligence and compassion, brought about by the instructions of Tehuty, who awakens and cleanses man's inner being.

The text also mentions that Hunefer has seen God's light in nature, which is born of yesterday, from the eastern side of heaven, and Hunefer recalls that the strength of this light is his strength. This passage is relevant to the Egyptian mythology, which says that Nut (heaven) swallows the Sun disk at the end of the day and gives birth to it on the second day, younger than yesterday. In other words, every new day contains a new life, and if anyone has a clear intention to change their life, even for the worse, this can be achieved. Hunefer indicates that this power of youth and regeneration, which comes every day through the rays of the Sun from the eastern side of heaven, is his power.

The text also mentions the four sons of Heru, or the four sons of light. These are the four essential inner organs, namely the lungs, the liver, the intestine, and the stomach, which are very important in the life of every human. They are not chemical particles and compositions of matter; the spirits that underlie them affect one's eternal life. All of one's actions in life are recorded in these organs, and so if the mundane desires in this life are stronger than the desire for life eternal, the person will not be able to collect their spiritual faculties and bodies together. Such an

A wooden Ka statue of the pharaoh Auib-re Hor. The Ka
is the desire body, dictating thought and ego.

The Khu is the universal spirit of God, which gives life to everything in the universe and exists in every single atom. The Ba is the human soul, which resides in the marrow of the bones and gives life. The Ka is the desire body, which resides in the small intestine. It dictates the individual's character, way of thinking, and ego. It is also called "double," since the conflict between the false self and the real self takes place within it. The Saah is the spirit body, which resides in the liver. It gives power, strength, vitality, genetic qualities, and protection.

The Kihibit is the astral body, which resides in the spleen and pancreas. It is also known as the light body, or design body, since it can take the same shape as each individual human being that it belongs to. This body is responsible for the individual's innocence and ability to learn from different realms of existence.

The Sekhem is the electromagnetic body, which circulates in and out of the human body, bringing in the five currents of earth energy to nourish the human soul. This body is responsible for the healing of disease. The physicians of ancient Egypt were, therefore, called the priests of Sekhemet.

The Eb is the heart body, which resides in the physical heart and the area between the heart and the solar plexus. The Ren is the sound body, which is comprised of the collective vibrations emitted by the inner organs and the individual's name, which is uttered by the person himself and other people in his life.

The Khat is the physical body, which has 12 main inner organs, 434 muscles, 101 joints, 206 bones, 12 main rivers of energy, 8 seas, many streams to connect them, and 22 vessels, which carry energy from the brain to the organs.

The elaborate and incredible structure of numbers that makes up the physical body contains an amazing meaning.

individual will, ultimately, be vanquished and their soul will not find any support. These four inner organs were, therefore, called the four supporters of heaven, or the supporters of the four cardinal points.

The human constitution, according to the Egyptian spiritual doctrines, is composed of nine bodies, each of which is located in a particular part of the physical body.

PLATE 10

We have 33 sutures in the skull, for example, the first three of which, on top of the head, fuse at the age of 22, while the rest progressively fuse at the ages of 28, 32, 36, 38, 42, and 46. The tissues of the spleen of the living human are renewed completely every 24 hours.

The entire universe is an arrangement of numbers and everything in the universe expresses its character through a specific number. All living things are capable of perceiving mathematical expressions. Numbers are both finite and infinite, and all numbers came from the Tpy Nu or the Monad, the principle of one. Numbers are only one branch of the science of mathematics.

Mathematics is the science that studies two major phenomena: multitude and magnitude. The study of multitude is divided into two main subjects: the relation of the part to itself (Arithmetic) and the relation of one part to other parts (Music). The study of magnitude is divided into two major subjects: stationary (Geometry) and movable, which again includes two subjects—Astronomy and Stereometry.

The ancient Egyptians utilized these sciences of mathematics to understand and learn more about the living human and the heavenly bodies (stars) and their influence upon earth and in rituals.

The Egyptian spiritual doctrines explain that the choices for liberation are, essentially, expressed through two paths. The first is the indirect path, or the path of Oser, also known as the long waterways of the West, or the southern path. This is the path of reincarnation. The second is the direct path, the path of Sokar, or the northern path, which is the path of perfection. The human soul depends on these other spiritual bodies in its salvation after death. If these spiritual bodies are not purified, they cannot enter the domain of heaven and the soul is lost in the Dwat (netherworld).

Bas-relief sculpture on a colonnade of the temple of Isis complex on the island of Philae on the River Nile.

The cat (Bast) was a symbol of joy and self-control,
an interesting juxtaposition of qualities.

Plates 10 and 11 of the Papyrus of Hunefer mention the seven spirits or powers in nature, which devour the enemies of Oser (good). These seven powers are represented in a universal way, in the form of Enuk, which is the self, hidden and concealed like the original creative powers. It is the "I," that is the collective intelligence of the nine bodies of the human being.

Mundane life, with its ever-present duality, evokes the need for the power, Mer, which is love. Love is the affinity for unity with the unknown or with God. Sekhem is the electromagnetic power, which circulates in and out of the human body, nourishing and regenerating the energy of the soul. Kheprer is the power that causes transformation, regeneration, evolution, becoming, and existence. Ab-Eb is

the desire of the heart, which causes the continuity of life. Tekh is the power that causes absorption. Without it, there would be no learning or continuity in life. Seshat-Sefex is the power of signature upon all creations. It is the outcome of all the previous six powers. We, therefore, find in nature seven colors, seven notes in music, seven vowels, a timespan of seven years for the renewal of the cells in the body, and seven vertebrae in the neck, whether in a man, giraffe, camel, or frog.

These seven powers are expressed specifically in the human flesh, in the form of the four essential inner organs, called the sons of Heru, and the grandsons of Heru, which are the other supporting inner organs within the human body, and these are the names that appear in the text. The text mentions that these seven organs are the true supporters of the principle of good in the human existence in this life. It also mentions that these are the same spirits that support the constellation of the Big Bear in northern heaven. The constellation of the Big Bear (Khepsh) is called the constellation of the thigh and also includes seven stars, representing those seven organs, the seven glands, and the seven major countries in the world.

The text mentions that the spirits that cause the destruction of sins exist in the constellation of the Small Bear (Ursa Minor) and they are reflected on earth through the law of harmony. Hunefer managed to vanquish his sins at a remote time, even as he was emerging from his mother's womb.

The seven spirits are also called the celestial ship of the north, and they cause the protection and purification of all good. Their power descends specifically between the hours of midnight and 6 AM, when they become active on earth. The head of these powerful spirits is Heru, the son of Oser and the avenger of his father, and the spiritual future of each soul

PLATE 10

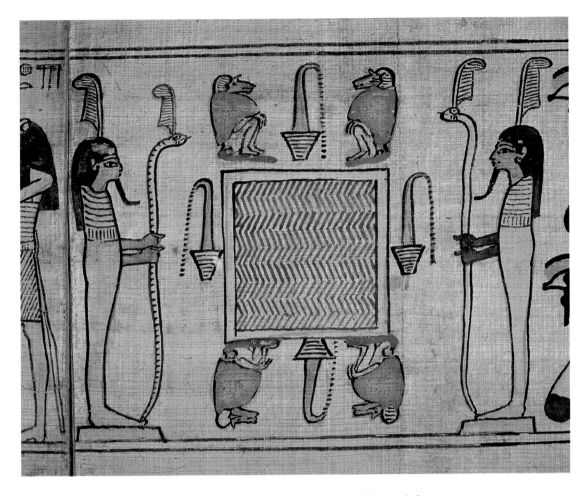

In this illustration, the human psyche is represented by a pool of water,
with a baboon at each corner representing the knowledge of the fire of life.

can only be acknowledged in truth, when the person steps beyond the realm of death into the Dwat (netherworld).

The text calls the spirits of light and justice *Thafy*. The root of this word implies purity and clarity and, even in the Semitic language, the roots of this word are still the same. These spirits of purification and clarity were caused by Heru, the son of Oser, at the beginning of time. They exist in the light of the Sun, the air, and the moisture, and also within the human being in different forms.

Finally Hunefer mentions that he is like the cat, which is constantly struggling to achieve joy and happiness. The cat is the symbol of self-control, since it does not resist motion, and therefore does not get hurt. It achieves its victory in the dreamland more than in awakening. When you look at a cat, it appears to be almost asleep for much of the time, but in its sleep, it is actually more awake. If you try to attack a cat while it sleeps, you will be surprised by its response and reflexes, which match the speed of light.

97

PLATE 11

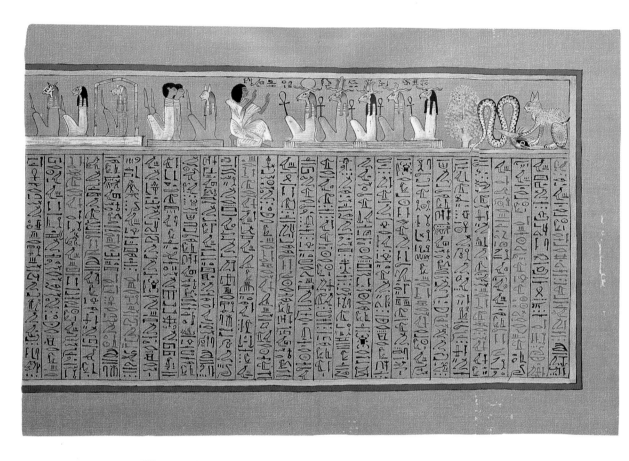

Illustrations

Plate 11 continues from Plate 10. The upper register begins on the left-hand side with a cow-headed symbol, indicating life-giving and eternal providence, a lion-headed symbol, representing day, another lion-headed symbol within a shrine, representing night, two symbols with human heads turned backward and a cat-headed symbol, representing joy. Then Hunefer emerges, in a kneeling posture, in front of Ra (Sun), Shu (air), Tefnut (moisture), Seb (earth), and Ba-N-Djed. Behind these laws, a cat is severing the head of the snake of darkness with a knife, beneath a persea tree. This represents the victory of Hunefer's soul, as the joyful, happy, and divine side of his soul emerges victorious over the dark side.

Translation

1 *The persea tree is near him in Eunu, on the night when the enemies of the master of limits are destroyed.* **2** What does this mean? *It is the divine cat, which is itself a being of light and is called Meau (cat) by the master of knowledge (Sa) himself, in truth. In other words, Shu gives the properties of earth to Hunefer, the*

PLATE 11

overseer of the royal cattle, who is united with Oser, victoriously. **3** As for the mountains of heaven by the persea tree near him in Eunu, the children of the impotent revolt were punished for what they did. **4** As for the night of the battle between good and evil, when it entered the eastern part of the sky, a great war took place in heaven and on earth to the limits. Hail, supporter of heaven, Shu, without equal among the natural laws! **5** Giving everlasting life for the shining spirits, deliver the royal scribe, Hunefer, who is united with Oser, victoriously, sailing over the pillars of Shu. Grant victory to the royal scribe of divine offering, Hunefer, who is united with Oser. **6** You bring the great hidden powers, shining between his eyebrows, like the two arms of the scales of justice on the night of judgment. **7** What does this mean? It is Enpu, the head of the divine chiefs who devour the enemies of the master of limits. **8** What does this mean? It is Heru, the reckoner who is endowed with knowledge. **9** It is the princes, who stand for the vision of the truth. **10** In other words, the royal scribe, overseer of the royal house, Hunefer, who is united with Oser, seeks to know the enemies of Oser, in order to destroy them in their abode, which revolves in the sky. **11** I know their names, from remote times, when the guiding light of Oser was sending invisible beams of light from his eye to clear the way, like the Nile, which is hidden. **12** I am strong upon earth and before the divine father, Oser, who effects the transformations of the soul. **13** These celestial beings fly with me, in the fellowship of the master of limits in his ordained transformation. **14** I achieved spiritual height (lit. flying as a divine falcon). I acquired physical perfection (lit. cackling as a goose). **15** I advance in eternity, like the rays of the Sun. **16**

What does this mean? It is light itself. **17** Oh! Deliver the royal scribe, overseer of the royal cattle, Hunefer, victorious from everyone who seizes the souls and eats the hearts of the living in disgust, using the power of fear and bursting out among his victims. **18** What does this mean? It is Suty (Satan), who uses false reasoning (lit. shining of mouth) and the intellect, but the true regeneration comes from Oser. In other words, the regeneration is from the light of God in nature. **19** Now, I can cause my own transformations. I carry the light of my awareness upon my forehead. Est, who is concealed, supports my action and I can see through the divine light of immortality. **20** Now, for those who rise up against me with evil, the power of darkness within them will destroy them.

A typical village to be found in modern Egypt. Here the houses are built right beside the River Nile.

Commentary

The text and illustrations in Plate 11 illustrate the sanctity of the persea tree of Eunu (Heliopolis). Beneath a persea tree, a cat, the symbol of solar power and the light of God in nature, severs the head of the snake of darkness. This indicates that good overcomes evil and that the power of earth gives life to those who follow the path of good. The text also mentions that the battle between good and evil extends to the limits of the stars in heaven and that the enemies of good and the people who killed Oser are punished for their *"impotent revolt."* In this battle, Set, or the devil, uses the power of fear, which is illusory, to rule his victims. He is described as using his *"shining of mouth,"* which implies that he uses false reasons, and *"movable of head,"* which implies that he uses his intellect. The text also mentions that the true regeneration comes only from Oser (Osiris), which is the power of good in nature. Innocence is the essence of all good and we are all protected, more by

100

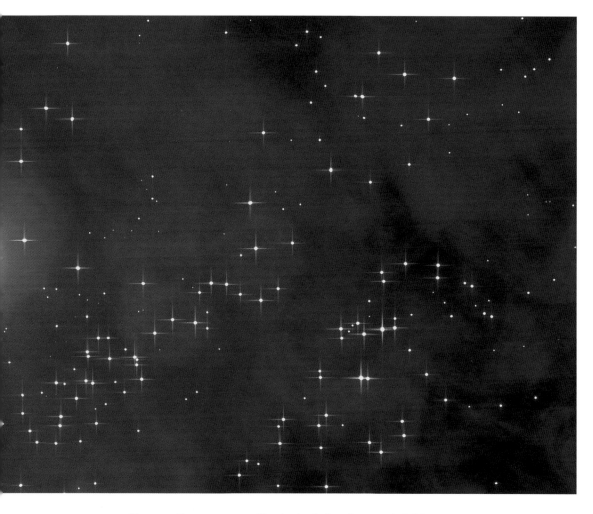

The stars of heaven were considered to be the breeding ground of all human souls.

our own innocence than by being clever. A soul that has lived with innocence in this life comes forth in the netherworld as an eternal child. In chapter 42 of *The Book of the Dead*, it says:

"*Neither men nor principles, glorified ones or damned, not generations past, present, or to come, can inflict any injury on him who comes forth and proceeds as the eternal child, the everlasting one.*"

The Plate ends with Hunefer proclaiming that he can bring about his own transformations now and that he carries the light of his awareness upon his forehead. He says that he is supported by the invisible power embodied in Est (Isis), and that he is able to see through the divine light of immortality. Hunefer concludes by saying that anyone who directs evil against him will be destroyed by their own feelings.

—4—

EXTRACTS
FROM THE BOOK
OF THE DEAD

EXTRACT FROM THE PAPYRUS OF ENHAI: PLATE 1

Translation

Behold, the singer of the hidden light (Emen), Enhai, who is united with Oser! She said: "May I drink water from the source of life, may I not be shut within the limits of my body, may I advance toward the sacred boat of life, and may I not be repulsed from my own boat."

The colonnade hall of the temple of Saqqara, which was the domain of the Egyptian sages.

Commentary

The ancient Egyptians symbolized someone who has never left the boundaries of their own town by a donkey, which implies ignorance. The town referred to here is the human body. Most humans are shut within the limits of their bodies, and therefore become like a donkey that carries the knowledge of eternal life on its back and exchanges it for a sip of water. In this extract, the lady Enhai, who was a singer and a priestess in the temple, prays that she will not be shut within the confines of her body. Material desires and lust create many limitations, but such limitations are ordained only for the limited.

105

EXTRACT FROM THE PAPYRUS OF ENHAI: PLATE 2

Translation

Tehuty, who was the master of the City of Eight, said: "I have come to you. I am Tehuty, your divine brother. I have come forth from the City of Eight and made my offerings in Eunu. I am glorious with your glories. I grow through your strength and your works of art are always in my mouth. I have come in order to bring you the truth, so that you may live thereby, rejoice therein, acquire union thereby, love therein, and achieve perfection thereby."

Est (Isis) and Nebt-Het (Nephthys) stand behind Oser (Osiris), who is seated on the throne of Egypt.

Commentary

This text indicates that the city of Tehuty (Hermes) was Hermopolis, which was known as the City of Eight because it was here that the eight foremothers and fathers of mankind lived. The text also indicates that Tehuty established his work of divine revelations in the city of Eunu, or Heliopolis.

Ancient Egypt had four centers of education: Eunu (Heliopolis), Net Xemenu (Hermopolis), Men-Nefer (Memphis), and Uast (Thebes). These four cities represent the four chambers of the heart. The divine revelation came forth through the City of Eunu, was established in the city of Men Nefer, explained in the city of Net Xemenu, and flourished in the city of Uast. Tehuty here calls all of mankind and points out that one can live only with the truth. All other ways lead to death.

Corinthian capitals decorate the tops of columns in the ruined Greco-Roman city of Hermopolis Magna. These ruins now stand in the modern Egyptian city of Ashmunein.

EXTRACT FROM THE PAPYRUS OF GERUSHER (*THE BOOK OF BREATHINGS*): COLUMN 1

Translation

The Book of Breathings of Tehuty is a means of protection for you. You should breathe through it every day and your eyes will see the rays of the Sun. The truth will speak for you before Oser and writings of the truth will always be upon your tongue. Heru, the avenger of his father, will protect your body and make your soul divine, like all the souls of the natural laws of light, who will make your soul live. The divine souls of the air will unite the passages of your nostrils.

Heru (Horus) leading the deceased to the judgment hall in the afterlife.

A stela depicting the deceased standing before Oser and Heru in the afterlife.

Commentary

The Egyptian sages established a system of breathing exercises, in order to make the human soul divine. This extract refers to the value of these living prayers (exercises). Breath is the key to life. If you breathe continually and consciously, you will never get ill; if you breathe deeply, you will never die. The Egyptian sages designed essential breathing exercises for the 12 senses (seeing, hearing, smelling, touching, tasting, feeling, transmission of ideas, telepathy, clear sight, spiritual discernment, intuition, and realization). The daily practice of these exercises was supposed to ultimately render the individual immortal.

EXTRACT FROM THE PAPYRUS OF GERUSHER: COLUMN 1

Translation

The beginning of The Book of Breathings. *Hail, Gerusher, son of Dashetyd, who is united with Oser! You are pure, your spiritual heart is pure, your chest is clean, your back is purified with water, your inner organs have been cleansed using herbs and salt, and none of your organs have any impurities left. Gerusher, son of Dashetyd, who is united with Oser, is purified in the pool of the Fields of Peace at the north of the Field of Grasshoppers. Uadyt and Nekhebet have purified you at the eighth hour of the day and the eighth hour of the night. Come then, Gerusher, son of Dashetyd, who is united with Oser, and enter the hall of the double truth. You are cleansed from all sins and oppositions and the stone of truth has become your sound body.*

Hail, Gerusher, son of Dashetyd, who is united with Oser! Enter into the underworld as a greatly purified man. The two principles of double truth have purified you in the great hall of justice. Your purification took place in the earthly domain and your organs have been made pure, starting from the sanctuary of life within your lungs. You see light, day and night. God granted you air and Ptah formed and molded your organs. Therefore, enter the horizon with light. The divine keepers receive your soul into the divine boat of Oser. They made your soul divine upon earth and they made you victorious in truth, for ever and ever.

The lady Enhai with a sistrum and a branch of lotus flowers, representing her ability to resist evil and give life.

The decorated entrance to the burial chamber of Emenhetep II, with a mural of the
king standing before Est (Isis), who is giving him life eternal.

An illustration depicting the different levels of the Sekhet-Earu (Fields of Peace), or the Elysian Fields.

XXXXXXXXXXXXXXXXXXXXXXXXXX

Commentary

The circulation of earth energy is one of five types of circulation, which affect our lives physically and spiritually. The subtle energy of earth enters the human body through the feet, hips, and kidneys, and has five currents. These currents mix with the energy generated by the soul (Ba), which resides in the marrow of the bones, feeding the 12 inner organs in a cycle during the hours of day and night. Each organ is fed for two hours. Er-Maat-N-F (the colon) is fed by the internal energy from 5.00–7.00 AM; Dua-Mut-F (the stomach) from 7.00–9.00 AM; Heqa (the spleen/pancreas) from 9.00–11.00 AM; Er-Maaty (the heart) from 11.00 AM–1.00 PM; Qeb-Sen-F (the intestine) from 1.00–3.00 PM; Er-Ren-F-Des-F (the urinary bladder) from 3.00–5.00 PM; Hnd-Hnd (the kidneys) from 5.00–7.00 PM; Kedt-Nu (the pericardium) from 7.00–9.00 PM; Ery-N-F-Nu-Et (the glandular system) from 9.00–11.00 PM; Aha-Shp-Aha (the gallbladder) from 11.00 PM–1.00 AM; Mesty (the liver) from 1.00–3.00 AM; and Hapi (the lungs) from 3.00–5.00 AM. Acts of purification and religious cleansing were, therefore, conducted at specific times, as mentioned in the extract, where cleansing took place at the eighth hour of the day and night.

The text mentions that Gerusher was purified in the pool of the Fields of Peace, at the north of the Field of Grasshoppers. The Fields of Peace are the waiting place for blessed souls and the fields of grasshoppers are the fields of the wise ones. The text also mentions that Gerusher entered the underworld as a greatly purified man and that he was purified by the two principles of double truth, which are Tehuty (Hermes) and Heru-Ur (Hercules or Horus the Great). Gerusher's purification took place upon earth and

he achieved the purification of his inner organs, beginning with the sanctuary of life within his lungs. This indicates the importance of breathing in the spiritual path of the soul. The text, therefore, indicates that Gerusher, because of his efforts upon earth to purify his inner organs, was invited by the divine keepers of the soul into the divine boat of Oser (Osiris). They made his soul divine when he was upon the earth and made him victorious in truth for evermore in the realm of the soul.

A typical cultivated field on the floodplain of the Nile in modern Egypt.

EXTRACT FROM THE PAPYRUS OF THE ROYAL MOTHER NEZEMT:

"The Negative Confessions" Chapter 25, Plate 5

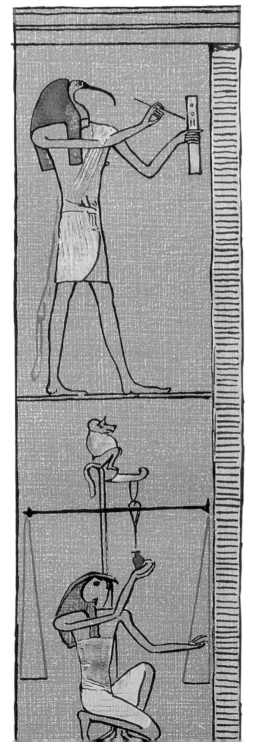

Translation

The victorious royal mother, Nezemt, who is united with Oser, says:

1. Hail, Usekht, who comes forth from Eunu.
   I have not committed sins.
2. Hail, Qenshest, who comes forth from Kher-Ahau.
   I have not robbed.
3. Hail, Eri-Tehuty, who comes forth from the City of Eight (Hermopolis).
   I have not stolen.
4. Hail, Hega-Khibit, who comes forth from Qerrt.
   I have not acted with violence.
5. Hail, Ha-Hera, who comes forth from Ra-Stet.
   I have not killed humans.
6. Hail, Rulty, who comes forth from heaven.
   I have not stolen offerings.
7. Hail, Maat-Fy-M-Seshet, who comes forth from Sekhem.
   I have not caused destruction.
8. Hail, Nebew, who comes forth from Khetkhet.
   I have not plundered the divine property of the temple.
9. Hail, Sedqeset, who comes forth from Het-Suten-Khenen.
   I have not committed falsehood.
10. Hail, Uadtu-Nesert, who comes forth from Het-Ka-Ptah.
    I have not plundered grain.

114

11. Hail, Qerty, who comes forth from Ementet.
    I have not cursed.

12. Hail, Hed-Ebhu, who comes forth from Ta-She.
    I have not transgressed.

13. Hail, Emy-Senty, who comes forth from the slaughterhouse.
    I have not slaughtered the divine cattle of the temple.

14. Hail, Emy-Besk, who comes forth from Maab.
    I have not done evil.

15. Hail, Nebt-Maat, who comes forth from Maaty.
    I have not plundered cultivated land.

16. Hail, Temmy, who comes forth from Best.
    I have not acted in lust.

17. Hail, Nadiu, who comes forth from Eunu (Heliopolis).
    I have not cursed anyone.

18. Hail, Nedty, who comes forth from Aty.
    I have not been angry without just cause.

19. Hail, Oammty, who comes forth from Khebt.
    I have not slept with the husband of any woman.

20. Hail, Maa-En-Af, who comes forth from Per-Emsu.
    I have not polluted myself.

21. Hail, Her-Peru, who comes forth from Amu.
    I have not acted with terror against any man.

22. Hail, Sekhemwit, who comes forth from Kheru.
    I have not plundered.

23. Hail, Shedu-Kheru, who comes forth from Uri.
    I have not acted with anger.

24. Hail, Nekhenu, who comes forth from Uasty.
    I have not turned a deaf ear to the words of righteousness and truth.

25. Hail, Sert-Kheru, who comes forth from Unes.
    I have not stirred up strife.

26. Hail, Djety, who comes forth from Shetawi.
    I have not caused anyone to weep.

27. Hail, Her-Fy-M-Ha-Tep-Fy-Ert-Fy-Dbw-Tep-F, who comes forth from Tebhw.
    I have not fornicated.

A painted limestone stela from Abydos
depicts an offering for the afterlife.

28. Hail, Tau-Rdy, who comes forth from the darkness.
I have not eaten my heart.

29. Hail, Kenmmty, who comes forth from Kenmmty.
I have not cursed anyone.

30. Hail, En-Hetepu, who comes forth from Zsau.
I have not exaggerated.

31. Hail, Nebt-Heri, who comes forth from Nedtw.
I have not judged anyone hastily.

32. Hail, Sedshui, who comes forth from Wdez.
I have not cut the hair and skin of divine animals.

33. Hail, Nebt-Abuy, who comes forth from Zsawty.
I have not raised my voice in speech.

34. Hail, Nefer-Tumm, who comes forth from Het-Ka-Ptah (Memphis).
I have not committed a sin and I have not done wrong.

35. Hail, Tum-Septy, who comes forth from Djedu.
I have not cursed royalty.

36. Hail, Erw-M-Eb-F, who comes forth from Tebuty.
I have not spoiled running water.

37. Hail, Enhwiw, who comes forth from Nu.
I have not acted with arrogance.

38. Hail, Hed-Rexty, who comes forth from Zsat.
I have not cursed divinity.

39. Hail, Nehebt-Nefert, who comes forth from his cavern.
I have not acted with false pride.

40. Hail, Nehebt-Ka, who comes forth from his cavern.
I have not acted scornfully.

41. Hail, Tseru-Tep, who comes forth from his shrine.
I have not increased my wealth, except by means of my own possessions.

42. Hail, Ena-F, who comes forth from...
I have not scorned the principle of my city.

Commentary

The 42 Negative Confessions were a forerunner of the Ten Commandments laid down by Moses. In the Egyptian Confessions, however, the responsibility of the individual is personal, whereas the Ten Commandments became imposed human law. In the Egyptian Confessions, therefore, the individual acknowledges that he has not killed, while in the Ten Commandments, it states, "Thou shalt not kill."

Confession 9 says, "I have not committed falsehood." This implies that the individual followed the ways of the truth, and if she did not know something, she would simply admit that she did not know. Today, we find half-knowledgeable people speaking with authority, as if they know everything, or fabricating factual information. When the leaders of Sparta visited the Oracle of Delphi, one of the questions they asked was when the world would end. The response was, "When the ignorant speaks about knowledge, the whore speaks about honor, and the tyrant speaks about justice."

Confession 10 says, "I have not plundered grain." This implies that the individual had not plundered cultivated land, which was the very first act of the devil, Set. Cultivated land was seen to represent the stars of heaven, while its grains and fruits are the sustenance and nourishment of the people on this earth. The act of plundering and destroying cultivated land, therefore, implies that the individual has actually lifted their hand in violence against heaven itself.

Modern Egyptian farmers, working in fields by the River Nile. Since the building of the Aswan Dam, farmers have used artificial fertilizers.

117

In Confession 19, it is written, "I have not slept with the husband of any woman." This implies that the individual lived her life with integrity and upheld the correct moral code. When someone commits an evil act of this nature, their own soul and spirits feel it, and it will lead, ultimately, to their own destruction—physically, mentally, and spiritually. It is impossible to acquire higher values by stealing, or divine pleasure by robbing. Divine joy and pleasures can be attained within the boundaries of one's own freedom, but when they extend to another person's freedom, they become oppression and an act of tyranny.

Confession 20 says, "I have not polluted myself," implying that the individual lived a clean and unpolluted life, eating the right foods and doing the right things. The human body is like a river. When acts of pollution are committed, the river of life is affected, causing impairment of the spiritual faculties, which, ultimately, leads to the loss of the soul in the spiritual realm.

Confession 24 says, "I have not turned a deaf ear to the words of righteousness and truth." This implies that the individual followed the words and instructions that were given by the truth. A question that has always been asked throughout the history of mankind is: "What is the truth?" The truth in this life is words, deeds, or thoughts that bring the individual closer to themselves and ultimately closer to God. Anything else, especially those actions which lead one in the opposite direction to the way of the truth, is seen to be falsehood. People are divided into those who have enough faith to make things happen, those with less faith who follow what happens, and plenty who wonder what on earth happened!

Confession 25 says, "I have not stirred up strife." This implies that the individual devoted her time and energy only to the development of good and never cultivated any bad seeds. It is very evident that, if someone is not part of the solution, they will always be part of the problem.

Confession 26 says, "I have not caused anyone to weep." This implies that the individual did not cause pain or suffering to any living thing on this earth, whether human, animal, bird, or reptile.

Confession 28 says, "I have not eaten my heart." This implies that the individual did not stand against her own feelings and inner nature, and was true to herself. People often act against their own feelings and the result is utter frustration and unhappiness.

Confession 35 says, "I have not cursed royalty." This implies that the individual respected royalty for what it is and acknowledged that its source is divine. Today, there is often a lack of respect for royalty, and many people expect its members to act as acrobats or behave like filmstars. In fact, I believe that the mere presence of royalty brings divine order to the rulership of a nation, without needing to do anything of particular merit in the physical or mundane realm. The absence of royalty implies the absence of divinity in the life of a nation, and the obliteration of royalty indicates obliteration of divine order within the human psyche. The slogan of the French revolution was, "Kill the last king with the intestine of the last priest." In other words, royalty and the priesthood were demolished at the same time and the result was spiritual bankruptcy, which I regard as the main ailment of our society today.

Confession 36 says, "I have not spoiled running water." Today, we all hear about ecology and the importance of protecting the environment, but too little continues to be done on a personal level. Most of the efforts that are made to safeguard the environment today are equivalent to someone trying to protect themselves from a hurricane using an umbrella! In ancient Egypt, the civil law stated that, if you cut a tree, you would be killed; if you spoiled running water, you would be killed; and if you killed an animal, you would be killed. The civil law preserved the environment and at the same time protected people from committing sins without knowledge.

Confession 40 says, "I have not acted scornfully," which means that the individual did not act in vengeance. Most of the time, our protection comes from our innocence. When you do not retaliate against someone who has done you wrong and you leave it to God, the retribution is far greater than you could ever have brought about yourself.

Confession 41 says, "I have not increased my wealth, except by means of my own possessions." This implies that the person gained her fortune by means of her own labor and not through stealing or trickery. As Rockefeller said, "Behind every great wealth, there is a great sin." Fortunes are accumulated by futile means and those people who earn the most money in society today are not the ones who are the most deserving of it. In other words, the distribution of wealth in modern times has no justice and one's merits are not necessarily expressed by how much one earns.

A richly decorated scene shows King Tut being anointed with sweet-smelling ungents by his wife.

EXTRACTS FROM THE PAPYRUS OF ANI, *Chapter 1 (Plate 5)*

Oser seated on his throne as the king of the afterlife, supported by the two sisters Est (Isis) and Nebt-Het (Nephthys).

Translation

1 *The beginning of the chapters of* The Book of Coming Forth by Day *and of praises and glorification of entrance into and exit out of the netherworld, shining in the beautiful West (Dwat).* **2** *This is to be said on the day of burial, upon going into the netherworld, after coming forth to life.* **3** *The scribe, Ani, beloved of Oser, said: "Homage to you, the head of Ementet!* **4** *Behold, Tehuty, the King of eternity! He is with me.* **5** *I am the great lord of the boat of life. I have fought for you.* **6** *I have become one with those laws of nature, the divine masters, who cause Oser to be victorious on the day of weighing words and deeds.* **7** *Oser, I am your advocate. I am one of those natural laws.* **8** *I was born from heaven and worked with the natural laws to shut away the enemies of Oser.* **9** *Heru, I am your advocate!* **10** *I fought for you and defeated your enemies, in your honor.* **11** *I am Tehuty, who makes Oser victorious over his enemies on* the day of weighing words and deeds in the dwelling place of the great ones in Eunu. **12** I am stability and the son of stability. **13** I was conceived in the town of stability (Djedu) and I was born in the same town. **14** I witnessed the mourners and wailers for Oser in Egypt, and Oser was made victorious over his enemies. **15** Ra and Tehuty ordained for Oser to be victorious over his enemies. **16** I was with Heru on the day when Oser, the still of heart, was clothed and washed, unbolting the door of hidden things in the land of Rastau. **17** I was with Heru, protecting the shoulder of Oser, which was left by Set in the city of Sekhem. **18** I went forth and came in peace out of the flames, on the day when the enemies of Oser were destroyed in Sekhem. **19** I was with Heru on the days of the festivals of Oser, making the offerings on the sixth day of the festival of Dnet in the city of Eunu. **20** I am the purity priest in the city of stability and I am the lion in the temple of Oser, elevating the earthly existence to heaven. **21** I can see in truth the hidden things in the spiritual path of Rastau. **22** I am able to read the ritual book of the soul in the city of stability. **23** I am the ritual priest in his glory. **24** I am the great chief of the service on the day of celebrating the coming of light and life by placing the Hennu boat of Sokar on the sledge. **25** I have received the honor of digging the divine foundation of the temple in the city of Suten-Khenen. **26** O you, who cause perfected souls to enter the house of Oser, may you cause the perfected soul of the scribe, Ani, to enter the house of Oser (the netherworld), victorious, with you.

Atum-Ra sending rays of life and prosperity to the deceased, who is offering the fruits of her labors in earthly life.

Commentary

The Papyrus of Ani was found at Thebes (Uast) in Egypt, and was bought by the British Museum in 1888. It measured 78 ft. (23.8 m.) in length by 1 ft. 3 in. (38 cm.) in width and is the longest Theban papyrus known to this day. The papyrus was much older than Ani, whose name was later inserted into spaces that had been left blank. Ani was a royal scribe, accountant of the temple offerings, governor of the granaries of the masters of the city of Abdu (Abydos), and the scribe of the offerings of the masters of the city of Thebes. The papyrus is undated but some scholars believe that it dates from 1200–1500 BCE.

The text of the Papyrus of Ani is composed of two major sections. The first section contains hymns to Ra and Oser, and the judgment scene with texts. The second section has 62 chapters. The arrangement of the chapters by Lepsius was adopted by the British Museum, but this arrangement is actually incorrect. For example, Chapter 1 in the original text was designated as Chapters 5 and 6 in Lepsius' arrangement, while Chapter 2 in the original text became his Chapter 18.

In these chapters, the deceased declares that he had followed the path of Sokar. This is the direct path to immortality, which does not involve the process of reincarnation. Ani, therefore, prays that he may be granted all that is everlasting and that he may become victorious through his own efforts. He declares that he gained control over his limbs and his spiritual bodies. He, therefore,

A stela representing the royal scribe traveling in his chariot. Painted limestone, c. 1550–1086 BCE.

overcame the limitations of distance and became one with the masters of eternity. He acquired knowledge during his lifetime through adherence to the truth. He will, therefore, be granted the fruits of his labor upon earth and be able to execute his will in the bond of truth as he pleases.

The beginning of *The Book of the Dead* is, as we can see, very ceremonial. It expresses the wish of the deceased to be united with Oser (Osiris), the ideal of every living human and the symbol of good. It catalogs the deeds of the deceased during his lifetime and expounds his worthiness to enter the abode of the blessed.

Plate 5 of the Papyrus of Ani is the beginning of the ceremonial praises for the entrance into the Dwat (netherworld), which should be recited on the day of burial. Ani acknowledges that he has become one with the laws of nature and declares that Tehuty (Hermes), the principle of knowledge, is with him. He indicates that he was born from heaven and that, during his life, he worked with the natural laws of existence. He says that, in the far beginning of time, he saw the life, death, and resurrection of Oser, and the victory of his son, Heru, over Set (Satan), and that, as a result of his efforts in life, he can see the hidden things in the spiritual realm. He also indicates that he was honored and participated in the digging of the divine foundation of the temple in the city of Suten-Khenen.

The Plate concludes with an entreaty for the masters who cause perfected souls to enter the house of Oser (the Dwat, or netherworld) to allow Ani to enter with the perfected soul in a victorious manner.

Chapter 1 of this papyrus is similar to Plates 6, 7, and 8 of the Papyrus of Hunefer. There are, however, more details in the Papyrus of Ani. The Papyrus of Hunefer is really considered to be a simplified version of the entire *Egyptian Book of the Dead*.

PLATE 6

The Mu dancers leading the deceased to his tomb.

Translation

27 *May he hear as you hear, may he see as you see, may he stand as you stand, and may he sit as you sit.* **28** *O givers of nourishment to the perfected souls in the house of Oser, give nourishment to the soul of Ani and make him victorious before all the laws of Abdu. Make him victorious with you!* **29** *O openers of the way and openers of the roads to the perfected souls in the house of Oser, open the way, therefore, for him.* **30** *Open, therefore, the roads to the soul of the scribe, Ani, the accountant of the divine offerings of all the natural laws, so that he may be victorious with you.* **31** *May he go in with confidence; may he come forth in peace from the house of Oser!* **32** *May he not be repulsed, may he not be turned back, may he go in as he pleases, may he come forth as he desires, and may he also be victorious!* **33** *May he become able to execute his command in the house of Oser! May he walk, may he speak with you, may he be a glorified soul with you, may he find no weaknesses there, and may the scales of justice grant him justice on the day of trial!"*

PLATE 6

1 *Chapter of giving the power of reason to the divine scribe, Ani, so that he may be victorious in the netherworld.* **2** *This is to be said: "I rise out of the egg in the hidden land.* **3** *May the power of reason be granted to me. May I be able to speak before the Great Principle and the master of the netherworld.* **4** *May my arm and hand not be repulsed by the dictates of any natural law.* **5** *I am Oser, master of the spiritual road of Rastau. Elevate the scribe, Ani, with the higher beings, who are at the top of the steps of evolution.* **6** *I have followed my heart's desire and come from the pool of double fire, after quenching it.* **7** *Homage to you, master of radiance, at the head of the great house, within the darkness of night!* **8** *I have come before you. I am glorious. I am pure. My actions during my life have supported you and I have taken the side of your divine ancestors.* **9** *Grant me the power of reason, so that I may use it and follow my heart's light in the darkness of night."*

1 *If this book is known and engraved in writing upon the coffin, the deceased will come forth by day in all the forms of existence that he pleases and he will go into his royal place and not be repulsed.* **2** *Nourishment and knowledge will be given to him upon the altar of Oser.* **3** *He will enter, with harmony, the Field of Peace.* **4** *If this order of the one in the city of stability is known, then he will be given life and reflections in stability.* **5** *He will be knowledgeable, as he was upon earth.* **6** *He will perform his will, millions of times, like those natural laws who are in the netherworld in the bond of truth (Karma). This will be granted for the scribe, Ani.*

A child acknowledging the names of the Egyptian kings, depicted in cartouches over the wall of a temple. From the temple of Seti I, Abydos.

Commentary

In Plate 6, an entreaty is made on Ani's behalf for nourishment to be granted for his soul, so that he may be brought victorious before the natural laws. There is also a plea for the doors of the house of Oser (the Dwat) to be opened before him and a request that he may not be repulsed or turned back and that he may do as he pleases.

The Plate moves on into sub-chapters, the first of which is the chapter of giving the power of reason to the divine scribe, Ani. The power of reason is given to the deceased, so that he may reply in his own defense, and it comes from the effort that he cultivated in his life in order to gain intelligence in the netherworld. Ani assumes the character of Oser, saying that he had followed his heart's desire and come forth from the pool of double fire after quenching it. This implies that he followed the knowledge or intelligence of the heart in his life, while the pool of double fire refers to the struggle between good and evil. He also declares that he had come thus far into the presence of Oser, having become glorious and having achieved purity, and that he had taken the side of Oser's divine ancestors. Then he entreats Oser to grant him the power of reason, so that he may follow his heart's light in the darkness of night.

The prayers and hymns contained in this Plate are to be memorized and engraved upon the coffin of the deceased, in order that the deceased may come forth by day and do as he pleases in the netherworld. The text indicates that all the advantages of these prayers are granted for the scribe, Ani, implying that he had memorized them.

Oser (Osiris) standing in the middle between Nekhebet and Uadyt, symbols of North and South Egypt, with the signs of infinity before and behind him.

126

PLATE 6

CHAPTER 2 (END OF PLATE 17)

The deceased traveling in the boat of light and truth as a purified spirit.

Translation

1 Chapter of preventing a person's soul from being shut up in the netherworld. **2** Ani said: "Hail, exalted one, who is adored; mighty of souls, mighty warrior, who is causing awe among all the natural laws, with light shining upon his mighty throne. **3** He makes the way for the universal spirit of God for the soul of Ani. **4** I have been blessed; I have been blessed with intelligence. I have made the way to the place of light and compassion." **5** If this chapter were known, the deceased would be provided with intelligence in the netherworld, and no door in the West would be shut for him in his coming and going in heaven.

1 Chapter of opening the tomb to the soul and astral body in coming forth by day and of gaining power over the legs. **2** *Ani said: "The place of restraint is opened to my soul, so that it may dwell there. I have found the guiding eye of Heru, establishing splendor on the forehead of light. The limitations of distance have* *disappeared and I am weightless.* **3** *I have made it to the Great Way. My members are rejuvenated.* **4** *I am Heru, the avenger of his father, bringing the double crown to the right place. The way of souls is opened to my soul."*

A censer used for ceremonial purposes in the form of a pharaoh making offerings in his sun barque. New Kingdom. c. 14th century BCE.

129

Commentary

The soul of the deceased would have been shut in the netherworld (Dwat), if it had not acquired sufficient intelligence in life to nourish it after death. At the conclusion of Plate 17, however, it is mentioned that knowledge of this particular chapter could prevent a soul from being subjected to this fate.

Ani praises Oser (Osiris), indicating that he has no equal among the natural laws. He acknowledges that he was blessed in his life, particularly in respect of his intelligence, and, as a result, that he made his way through to the land of light and compassion. All closed doors were opened for his soul and he found guidance in the eye of Heru, son of Oser, or the solar path. His astral body, therefore, was nourished and he became weightless, allowing him to travel with ease, free from the limitations of distance. All of

An interior view of the murals in the tomb of Cheti, 12th dynasty, c. 1950 BCE.

The deceased standing before the Benu bird (phoenix), the symbol of reincarnation. To the right, Enpu (Anubis) blesses the mummy of the deceased. A mural from the tomb of Sennedjem, 12th century BCE.

his members, which implies the supporting spiritual bodies of his soul, were rejuvenated and, ultimately, the way of the blessed souls was opened to him. The physical body of the human being is resurrected after entering the tomb, in the form of the universal spiritual body, or Khu. This resurrection can only be achieved through divine efforts performed in the individual's life. As a result, the person rises above the mount of glory, declaring that they have established splendors, that limitations of distance have disappeared, and that they have become weightless. The human members of the universal spiritual body, which resemble the physical members of the earthly body in shape, are in reality a rejuvenation of them. The person, therefore, achieves the ultimate quality of perfection and is united with Heru, who is the symbol of the savior, who showed souls the way to perfection; not necessarily by carrying them across, since they have to carry themselves, with the application of conscious effort.

PLATE 18

The deceased and his wife standing in adoration before the gate to the afterlife.

Translation

5 *My soul sees the Great Principle within the boat of light on the day of souls.* **6** *My soul is in front, among those who reckon the years. The eye of Heru has delivered my soul for me, which established my splendor on the forehead of light, upon the faces of those who reside in the body of Oser.* **7** *May my soul become free, may my astral body become united, may a way open for my soul and for my astral body! May my soul see the Great Principle within the shrine, on the day of the judgment of souls; may my soul repeat the words of Oser!* **8** *May the hidden beings in the hidden dwellings do me no evil or turn away their path from me for I possess their hearts.* **9** *May my Ba (soul) and my Khu (universal spirit) be provided with protection against all evil guidance!* **10** *May I sit among the great ones, who dwell in their divine places!* **11** *May I meet no restraint of my limbs, my soul, and my astral body from the ones who possess heaven!* **12** *If this chapter were known by the deceased, his soul would meet no restraint.*

PLATE 18

1 *Chapter of walking with the two legs and of coming forth upon earth.* **2** *Ani said: "You have done your divine works of Sokar (repeat this twice), within his dwelling place and within my legs in the netherworld.* **3** *I shine above the leg of heaven. I come forth from heaven; I have come to rest by the side of the divine spirits.* **4** *Hail! I am helpless (repeat this twice). I walk along. I am helpless and motionless in the presence of the devourer of the dead in the netherworld. May Ani become victorious in peace!"*

1 *Chapter of passing through Ementet and of coming forth by day.* **2** *Ani said: "Eunu is open; the face of Tehuty is hidden; the eye of Heru is perfect. I have delivered the eye of Heru, shining with splendor on the forehead of light, the father of all the natural laws.* **3** *I am Oser, who dwells in Ementet. Oser knows his time. He does not exist with evil there and I shall not exist there either.* **4** *I am the moon among the natural laws. I shall not vanish. I shall stand up then for Heru, who has counted me among the laws."*

1 *Chapter of coming forth by day and of living after death.* **2** *Ani said: "Hail, the shining one from the moon! Hail, the shining one from the moon! Let Ani, who is united with Oser, come forth among your multitudes. Let him be established among the shining spirits and let the underworld be opened to him."* **3** *Behold Ani, who is unified with Oser! He shall come forth by day to do his will among the living.*

1 *Chapter of coming forth by day, after having traversed the tomb.* **2** *Ani said: "Hail, mighty soul of valor! Behold! I am here; I have come; I can truly see; I have traversed the netherworld; I have truly seen my father, Oser. I have dispelled darkness; I am his beloved. I have come, so that I may see my great father, Oser. I have stabbed the heart of evil and performed duties for my father, Oser.* **3** *I have opened for myself every way in heaven and on earth. I am a son, who loves his father, Oser. I have become royal, I have become glorious, I am provided with all that I need.* **4** *Hail to every natural law and shining being! May you make a way for me! I am the one who is identified with Oser, Ani, Ani triumphant."*

A sculpture of a sphinx at the temple of Ramses II stands partially submerged in the waters of the River Nile at Aswan.

133

A boat representing the moon as the island of the blessed. This silver boat model
was found in the intact tomb of Queen Anhotep, 1550 BCE.

1 *Chapter of bringing a man from the netherworld to see his house upon earth.* **2** *Ani, who is identified with Oser, said: "I am the lion coming forth with strides. I have labored and I have achieved my objectives (repeat this twice).* **3** *I am the eye of Heru. I have opened my third eye on time and I have arrived at the Fields of Peace, so let Ani, who is identified with Oser, advance in peace!"*

1 *Another chapter of coming forth by day, of a man against his enemies in the netherworld.* **2** *I have split heaven, I have passed through the horizon, I have traversed earth, following Oser's footsteps.* **3** *I have gained control over my spiritual bodies and I have become mighty because, behold! I was provided with Oser's millions of enchantments. I digest what I learn and absorb what I comprehend.* **4** *Behold, divine principle, the lord of the netherworld! May you grant me all that is everlasting! May Ani, who is identified with Oser, become victorious with his own efforts!*

1 *An adoration to the light of God, when it rises on the horizon and sets, giving life.* **2** *Ani, who is identified with Oser, said: "Homage to you, light of God in nature, when you rise and set, as the light of the two horizons."*

PLATE 18

Commentary

Plate 18 speaks of the deliverance of the soul after death, when Ani's soul has come face-to-face with the truth. It identifies Ani's soul with the eye of Heru, son of Oser (Osiris), and ends by stating that Ani has gained control over his spiritual bodies and has, therefore, become mighty, pointing out that Ani's final reward has resulted from his comprehension and obedience to the truth.

The true title of *The Book of the Dead* should be *The Chapters of Coming Forth in the Light of the Truth*. All diseases in life arise from an inability to face the truth. It is important to know that the source of life expresses itself through different forms, appearing as a source of nourishment, for example, in the element of water, in vegetation, and in fish. It also materializes through breath, which gives life. *The Book of the Dead* provides a way to achieve freedom from damnation and acquire final salvation. Its opening chapter is described as the words of truth, which bring about resurrection on the mount of glory. The closing chapters show the deceased upon the summit of attainment, united with the lords of eternity. The mouth of the deceased was closed by death, but it is opened for him again with the help of Ptah, Tum, son of Ptah, and Tehuty (Hermes).

In chapter 133 of *The Book of the Dead*, it says, "*O Teta, you have raised up your head for your bones and you have raised up your bones for your head.*" The bones here indicate the body, or earth, and the head indicates the soul, or heaven. The ancient Egyptians mummified the dead body to preserve it from corruption, as a mark of respect for the efforts made by the deceased during their lifetime in the pursuit of immortality; efforts that were respected by the

The right eye, the symbol of the sun, giving the fire of life to the souls of all creatures. From the tomb of Pashedu.

135

whole society. Bodies were not mummified because of a belief in physical resurrection, but rather as an expression of acknowledgment from the deceased's relatives and friends and the entire society of the individual's divine salvation for everlasting life. The dead body was, therefore, swathed in extraordinarily long bandages of linen, without seams, as a representation of this everlasting life.

The swathed corpse was called "Krst," which is the root of the Latin word *corpus* (dead body), the Greek *kreas* (human body), the Gaelic and Irish *Cras* (body), and the English "corpse." It is also the root of the word "Christ." The swathed body expresses the concept that action is no longer performed by means of the physical body but by the perfected body in a spiritual form, which is called "Khu." The word "Krst" refers to Christ in the context of a ritual of baptism, which was performed in order to purify the body by cleansing it with water and anointing it with oil. This expressed the elevation of the dead body into a "Saah," or spiritual body, pure and perfect.

The Egyptian mythology is, in reality, an astro-mythology, which tells the story of the struggle between good and evil, in heaven and upon earth. The story of Oser (Osiris) reflects this struggle in detail. Oser was murdered by his brother, Set (Satan), and, when Oser was brought back to life by his wife and companion, Est (Isis), Set and his followers, in the darkness of night, found the body of Oser again and dismembered it, cutting it into 14 pieces. The 14 pieces of Oser's body represent the phases of the Moon. Tehuty (Hermes), in the form of the Moon (which is the symbol of knowledge since it reflects the light of the Sun, giving life in the middle of darkness, which is ignorance), vanquished the powers of darkness, in conjunction with the stars of heaven, referred to as the children of light. The ancient Egyptians, therefore, celebrated ten great mysteries in ten festivals held on ten different nights of the year. The first night was the Night of Esht-F-Khu, or the Night of the Last Supper, held on the last day of the old year and followed by the Night of the Evening Meal, held on the first day of the new year. In these two festivals, food and offerings were laid upon the altars to celebrate the sacrifice that Oser made of himself. The Night of the Last Supper represents the night when Oser was slain by Set, with the help of the 72 conspirators. It is also the night of the great battle, in which Tehuty (the Moon) and the children of light (stars) vanquished darkness.

The second festival was the Night of Erecting the Djed column, which is the symbol of Oser, or the body of good. The Djed column was placed flat on the floor, representing the dead body of Oser. As part of the ceremony, the King pulled the Djed column upright from one side, helped by the priests, who pushed it from the other side, until it stood erect, as the symbol of the resurrection of Oser in the form of his son, Heru, the King of Egypt.

The third festival was the festival of the Night of Restoring the Eyesight of Heru, the son of Oser. During this ceremony every man and woman anointed their eyes with antimony (kohl).

The fourth festival was the Festival of Erecting the Pavilion of Heru and raising him to the throne of his father. Four pillars, representing the foundation of the human kingdom, were erected during that feast.

The fifth festival was the festival of the Night of the Drop, when one of Est's tears fell into the Nile, giving it warmth and life, as she did with her husband, Oser, by brooding over his body to give him warmth and vitality. This festival was held on the 11th day of the month of Paoni (June 17th). Even today, the Egyptians believe that, if a person is lucky enough to drink from the water of the Nile

PLATE 18

Feluccas sailing down the Nile in modern Egypt. The felucca is
designed so that it can sail in the slightest breeze.

in the particular hour of the night when that tear of Est dropped, they would be granted incredible physical and spiritual strength and their life would be renewed.

The sixth festival was the festival of the Night of Weighing Words and Deeds. This was the night on which the great festival of Saq-Er-E took place, when Oser and Est were reunited after their long separation.

The seventh festival was the festival of the Night of Judging the Wicked Enemies of Oser, when his enemies were defeated once more.

The eighth festival was the festival of the Night of Ploughing the Earth, when the enemies of Oser were slaughtered and their blood manured the earth.

The ninth festival was the festival of the Night of the Secret Ceremonies of Oser, when the dismembered pieces of Oser's body were gathered, collected, and bound together. The ritual performed on this day was the planting of corn seed in a pottery container shaped like the body of Oser, from which corn would spring out as a symbol of life overcoming death.

The tenth festival was the festival of the Night of Enpu (Anubis), the embalmer, who stands like a wall between the visible and invisible.

The chapter of these ten festivals of the mystery nights was recited in order to purify the deceased to prepare them to come forth in the light of truth.

Afterword

The Egyptian texts describe Oser (Osiris) as the giver of himself, as the food that will never perish. They also say that Oser was eaten as the bull of eternity, who gave his blood and flesh as sustenance for humanity. Oser was redeemed and resurrected in the form of his son, Heru, whose name is the root of the English word "hero," and he became the ideal for every living man in ancient Egypt.

The Egyptian salvation is purely personal and requires that everyone should learn how to survive on their own. They would not, therefore, need a redeemer to save them from something that would never happen. Every person makes their own fate and no one else is to blame. The Egyptian religion teaches that Heru, the son of Oser, did not come to save sinners who had not taken the trouble to save themselves in the first place. He came to justify the righteous.

Dr. Ramses Seleem.

Modern religions do not place this same emphasis on the notion of personal responsibility. Christians, for example, believe that Jesus came to redeem their sins, and died for humankind on the cross. But the Egyptian view is that no one can redeem the sins of others.

I believe that only in the old Egyptian texts do we find the truth—a religion built upon natural laws, not upon the life of an individual; the laws of nature are the true language and book of God. Did you ever plant a mango seed, that sprung up as wheat? The Sun rises from the east and sets in the west. Could anyone do the opposite?

Life, Prosperity, and Health.

With showers of blessings,

Dr. Ramses Seleem
London, 2000

GLOSSARY

Atlantis: The Egyptian name for Atlantis was "Etelenty," which means "the land that has been divided and submerged by water." Atlantis is the Greek name for this island, which used to be in the middle of the Atlantic ocean. It is where God created the very first humans.

Atum-Ra: One of the names for "God" in ancient Egypt. "Atum" means "end" and "beginning" and "Ra" means "light." "Atum-Ra," therefore, means "the beginning and end of light."

Djed: The column that represents the spinal cord of Oser (Osiris) or the axis of all good. It represents the four elementary systems in the human body: muscular, skeletal, cardiovascular, and nervous systems.

Dwat: The intermediary world (netherworld), or the purgatory state, between the kingdoms of Ta (earth) and Nut (heaven).

Emen and Emenet: One of the four couples who were created in Atlantis (Etelenty) as the forefathers and mothers of humankind. Emen (masculine) and Emenet (feminine) were the father and mother of the Egyptian race and migrated to Egypt along with the priesthood of Atlantis in c. 50,000 BCE.

Emen-Ra: Another name for "God" in ancient Egypt. "Emen" means "hidden" and "Ra" means "light." "Emen-Ra," therefore, means "the hidden light."

Enpu (Anubis): The son of Nebt-Het (Nephthys), who was reared and raised by a female greyhound. He became the guardian of the secret knowledge and the entry to the afterworld. He was the embalmer who embalmed the body of Oser (Osiris) and was called "the wall that stands between the visible and invisible."

Heh and Hehet: One of the four couples who were created in Atlantis as the forefathers and mothers of humankind. Het and Hehet were the father and mother of the Oriental race.

Heru-Sheriu (Horus the Younger): The son of Oser (Osiris) and Est (Isis), the savior of good and the redeemer of the good deeds of Oser to all mankind. He became the King of Egypt and all the kings of Egypt after him were an extension of him.

Kek and Keket: One of the four couples who were created in Atlantis as the forefathers and mothers of mankind. Kek and Keket were the father and mother of the black race and were the first to migrate from Atlantis and Africa.

Khnemu: One of the immortals of Atlantis, who migrated to Egypt and settled in Eunu (Heliopolis). He was the first master builder in the world and his works, which included the pyramids of Giza and many of the Egyptian temples, are still regarded with admiration today as objects of wonder.

Medu-Netru: This is the name of the ancient Egyptian language and means "words which convey the natural laws." The Greeks called the Medu-Netru "hieroglyphs," which means "sacred carvings."

Men-Nefer: A city located south of modern Cairo. It was the capital of ancient Egypt for thousands of years. The Greeks called this city Memphis.

Net-Tehuty: A city in middle Egypt that was the home town of Tehuty (Hermes) and the Eight Primordials (the forefathers and mothers of mankind). The Greeks called it Hermopolis, or the city of Hermes.

Neter: Masculine principle or law, which exists in nature in every form. It is similar to yang in Chinese philosophy.

Netrit: Feminine principle or law, which exists in nature in every form. It is similar to yin in Chinese philosophy.

Nine bodies: Khu, the universal spirit of God—this spirit gives life to everything in the universe; Ba, the human soul; Ka, the desire body; Saah, the spirit body; Kihibit, the astral body; Sekhem, the electromagnetic body; Eb, the heart body; Ren, the sound body. Khat, the physical body.

Nu (water of chaos): The third creative power in the triangle of the power of creation. God comes as the head of this triangle, then the sound uttered by Him to create, followed by the water of Nu, from which all creations came, with the exception of mankind.

Nun and Nunit: One of the four couples who were created in Atlantis as the forefathers and mothers of mankind. Nun and Nunit were the father and mother of the European race.

Ptah: One of the immortals of Atlantis, who migrated to Egypt in c. 50,000 BCE. He settled in Memphis and ruled Egypt for 9,000 years.

Paut: The nine natural laws of existence, which exist in the character of every human being. They are Shu (air), Tefnut (moisture), Seb (earth), Nut (heaven), Oser (Osiris), Heru-Ur (Hercules), Set (Satan), Est (Isis), and Nebt-Het (Nephthys.)

Ra: The light of God in nature, which comes to us through the right eye of God, the Sun.

Rastau: The entry to the Dwat (see above).

Sekhet-Earu: The Garden of Reeds, where peace and knowledge are the main features. It is the portion of heaven where enlightened souls dwell.

Sekhet-Hetep: The Fields of Peace, adjacent to Sekhet-Earu. These are two different levels of the spiritual realm of existence.

Sokar (Seker): The symbolic expression of the direct path to immortality.

Tehuty (Hermes): The founder of all knowledge, educator of all mankind, writer of the sacred books, which include all that was, all that is, and all that will be.

141

INDEX

A

Abu Simbel 85
Abydos 88
afterlife 112, 115, 132
Anhotep, Queen, tomb of 134
Amun, temple of 65, 91
Ani, Papyrus of 120–37
animal symbols 38–9
Ankh symbol 41
Anubis see Enpu
Atum-Ra 19, 20, 21, 54, 121, 140

B

"Ba" bird 83, 94
Bast (sacred cat) 38, 96, 97
Benu bird (phoenix) 83, 112, 131
Bey, Mariette 19
Big Bear constellation 96
black mirror 66, 67
Book of Breathings 108–13
breathing exercises 108–13
Budge, Wallis 17

C

Cheti, tomb of 130
City of Eight 106, 107, 114
cleansing 65–7, 113
Confessions, Negative 114–19
Creation 16–22, 40, 55
crocodile 36, 37, 37, 38

D

Dashetyd 110
de Rougé, E. 18–19
death 28–31, 70
Dendera 17
Dezgreg 63
Dezmaa 63
Djed 23, 41, 50, 77, 136, 140
Dwat 10, 12, 28, 140

Papyrus of Ani 120, 130, 133, 134
Papyrus of Hunefer 62, 63, 70, 77, 85, 88

E

Eaau 16, 54
earth energy circulation 113
Eb 94
education 64, 107
eight primordial humans 21, 22, 140
Emen and Emenet 21, 22, 140
Emen-Ra 16, 20, 48, 54, 140
Emenhetep II 111
Ementet 13, 14, 133
Enhai 104–7, 110
Enneagram 20
Enpu (Anubis) 14, 29, 68, 69, 74, 79, 137
Est 95, 111, 120
    Great Paut 26–7, 27
    Papyrus of Enhai 106
    Papyrus of Hunefer 50, 60–1, 72–3, 72, 84–5
    ten festivals 136, 137
Etelenty 21, 22, 59
eternity 10, 55
Eunu, city of 23–7, 98, 99, 100, 106, 107
evil 60, 63, 77, 89, 136

F

faith 54, 55
festivals, ten 136–7
frog 39

G

Generic Version Number One 33
Gerusher, Papyrus of 108–13
God 16–22, 53, 54, 55, 85
    see also Atum-Ra; Eaau; Emen-Ra
grasshopper 39, 110, 113
Great Nine Laws see Paut Netru

H

Hathor temple 52–3
healing 64, 77
Heh and Hehet 21, 140
Heliopolitan Version 32–3
Her-M-Akhety (the sphinx) 25, 25
Hermopolis Magna 107
Heru
    battles with Set 60
    eye of 86, 86, 90, 90
    four sons of 72, 72
    judgment of Hunefer 69, 70
    light and justice 92, 93
    salvation 138
Heru-Sheriu 15, 15, 27, 57, 60, 140
Heru-Ur 25, 57, 60
Horus, temple of 80–1
Hunefer 47–101, 48, 132

I

ignorance 15
immortality 64, 67
insects 39, 42, 110, 113
Isis see Est

J

judgment 13, 28–9, 68, 68, 69, 70

K

Ka 44, 62–3, 94, 94
Karnak 54, 65, 66–7, 69, 73, 84
Kek and Keket 21, 141
Kha-M-Hat 9
Khat 94
Kher-Heb 78, 78, 79
Khnemu 21, 22, 140
Khu 62, 94, 131, 132
Kihibit 94
knowledge 15
Krst (swathed corpse) 136

L

language, Medu-Netru 35–45
lions 39, 42–3
lotus flower 49

M

Maat-Men-Ra, King (Seti I) 47, 48, 49,
    56, 68
Medu-Netru 32, 33, 35–45, 141
Meidum, Egypt 61
Meskhent 31
monotheism 53
mouth, opening the 78, 79, 80
Mu dancers 124
mummification 14, 135–6

N

names, God 54
Nasha 48, 49, 49, 86, 87, 132
Nebt-Het (Nephthys) 24
    Great Paut 27
    Papyrus of Ani 120
    Papyrus of Enhai 106
    Papyrus of Hunefer 50, 72, 72, 73,
    84, 85
Negative Confessions 114–19
Nekhebet 126–7
Nephthys see Nebt-Het
Neserser 31
Net Xemenu, city of 107
Neter 11, 16, 141
netherworld see Dwat
Netrit 11, 16, 141
Netru 20
Nezemt, Royal Mother 114–19
Nile, river 58, 60, 116–17, 137
nine bodies 94, 96, 141
nine principles 51
Nun and Nunit 21, 22, 141
Nu (instrument) 78, 79
Nu (water of chaos) 20, 21, 51, 85, 141
numbers 94, 95
Nut (heaven) 10, 11, 24, 28, 93

P

Papyri
    Ani 10, 120–37
    Enhai 104–7
    Gerusher 108–13
    Hunefer 47–101, 48
    Royal Mother Nezemt 114–19
Paut Netru 20, 23–7
personality 63, 64
Plato 12, 13
Ptah 12, 13, 21, 22, 141
purification 65–7, 113
pyramids 32–3, 32–3

R

Ra 18, 20, 40, 90, 90
Ra-Heru-Akhety (Mars) 50
Rastau 31, 75, 76, 77, 88, 89, 140
reincarnation 70, 84
Ren 94
Renutt 31
Royal Mother Nezemt 114–19

S

Saah 40, 62, 94, 136
Saite Version 33
salvation 14, 15, 64, 135, 138
Saqqara 22, 32–3, 32–3, 105
scarab 39, 39, 42
Seb (earth) 24, 58
Sebek 37, 37
Sekeh, tomb of 30
Sekhem 94, 96
Sekhet-Hetep 70, 89
Sektet boat 51
Sennedjem, tomb of 131
serpent of darkness 38
Serqet (goddess) 29
Set (Satan) 25, 27, 59, 60, 89, 100
Seti I, temple of 125
seven spirits 92, 96
Shu 23, 38, 57
six pillars of healing 64, 77

snake 35, 36, 38, 39, 98
Sokar, path of 77, 123, 133, 141
sphinxes 25, 25, 73, 133
suffering 43
Sun 92–3, 93
    see also Ra

T

Ta (earth) 10, 28
Tefnut (moisture) 23, 38
Tehuty (Hermes) 45, 141
    city of 106, 107, 107
    eight primordials 21, 22
    God concept 54
    justice/judgment 10, 13, 13
    Papyrus of Hunefer 56, 60–3, 69, 70,
    90, 90, 91
Ten Commandments 117
ten festivals 136–7
Thafy 97
Theban Version 33
third eye 45, 134
Thutmose I 41
Thutmose III, tomb mural 44
triangle of earth 64, 65, 67
truth 118, 135, 138
Tut, King 119
Tut-Anx-Emen, King 28

U

Uadyt 126–7
Uast symbol 41

V

viper 39
vision 44–5, 134, 135

W

water cow 38
white mirror 66–7

Y

Ystorrynau 36

AUTHOR BIOGRAPHY

Ramses Seleem began to learn from a very early age with the members of UNNUT (the openers of heaven). The study involved not only the "classroom" subjects,which included religion, hieroglyphs, astrology, mathematics, philosophy, and natural medicine, but also physical culture. This contained seven main branches: SESH (stretching), SESENTI (breathing), KHENTU (postures), USERT (power exercises), SEBEK-KHA (warrior training), UDAU (sound exercises), and BAAU (glandular exercises). This study lasted for 25 years and comprised eight hours of physical training and four hours of theory a day, which had to be fitted in with Dr. Seleem's normal school education. It must be borne in mind that, because of the turmoil caused by the collapse of the Egyptian Empire and the invasions of Assyrians, Persians, Greeks, Romans, Christians, Turks, and Arabs, the people of Egypt today comprises 90 percent Muslims, 8 percent Coptic Christians, and only 2 percent Egyptians. Of this 2 percent, only half have any connection with the original tradition, and this 1 percent never appear in public. As a consequence, the ancient knowledge is effectively closed to scholars and, in fact, went underground 2,500 years ago. Dr. Seleem then enrolled in the Economics and Political Science Faculty of Cairo University, where he studied for a BSc degree. He then went on to obtain a Masters degree and then a doctorate in Egyptian history, gaining his PhD. After completing his military service, Dr. Seleem travelled to the United States, where he set up his own academy called the Egyptian Physical Culture Association. After twelve successful years, he decided to teach in other countries, and settled briefly in Australia, South Africa, and Holland, where he appeared on many television and radio programs, discussing the ancient Egyptian way of life. He also featured in numerous magazines and newspapers. Since 1996, Dr. Seleem has been living in London. He is principal of the Sia Academy, where he has taught and lectured for the last three years, and has appeared on MBC TV and has been interviewed by a number of leading periodicals, including the *Sunday Times Magazine*, *Red*, *What's On in London*, and *Marie Claire*. During this time he has written a screenplay called *The Pharaoh's Warrior*, a textbook on medicine entitled *The Ancient Egyptian Natural Medicine*, and an introduction to the ancient Egyptian tradition called *Return to the Source: Egypt*. He has also perfected an entirely new computer program as a word processor for Egyptian hieroglyphs. For more information about ancient Egyptian culture please contact:

Dr. Ramses Seleem

Tel/Fax: +44 20 7737 2260

Email: siaacademy@netscapeonline.co.uk

PICTURE CREDITS

The publishers would like to thank the following for permission to reproduce copyright material: AKG, London: pp. 54 (Robert O'Dea), 85 (Henning Bock), 96 (Norbert Schammel College, New York), 130 (François Guenet); AKG, London/Erich Lessing: pp. 13, 121 (Musée du Louvre, Paris), 19, 23 (Museo Egiziano, Turin), 24, 25, 28, 37, 38, 63, 109 (Egyptian Museum /Staatliche Museen Preussischer Kulturbesitz, Berlin), 124, 129 (National Maritime Museum, Haifa), 131; AKG/Erich Lessing (Kunsthistorisches Museum, Vienna): pp. 16, 30, 88, 97; The Art Archive: pp. 40, 115; Corbis: pp. 6–7, 57 (Farell Grahan), 11 (Charles and Josette Lenars), 17, 26–7 (Vanni Archive), 20, 107, 133 (Roger Wood), 23 (Historical Picture Archive), 42–3 (Earl and Nazima Kowall), 46–7 (Michael Nicholson), 58 (Jonathen Blair), 69 (John Jones,Cordaiy Photo Library), 75, 76, 80–1 (Ludovic Maisant), 91 (Stephanie Colasanti), 94 (Archivo Iconografico, S.A.), 95 (Adam Woolfitt), 102–3 (Paul Almasy), 105 (Wolfgang Kaehler), 113 (Stephan Widstrand), 134 (Fulvio Roiter); Corbis/Gianni Dagli Orti: 12, 29, 39, 41, 44, 70, 111, 122, 126–7, 135; Stone-GettyOne: 8–9, 15, 22, 32–3, 34–5, 36, 50–1, 52–3, 61, 65, 66–7, 71, 73, 84, 87, 92–3, 99, 100–1, 116–7, 137, 139; The Stock Market, London: 18.